Prayers and Meditations

The Mother

Prayers
and
Meditations

Sri Aurobindo Ashram, Pondicherry

Originally Published in 1932 as
Prières et Méditations de la Mère

Complete English translation
First Edition: 1948
Second Edition (new translation): 1979
Third Edition: 2003
Fifth Impression: 2005

Rs. 160.00
ISBN 81-7058-700-X
© Sri Aurobindo Ashram Trust 1948, 1979, 2003
Published by Sri Aurobindo Ashram Publication Department,
Pondicherry - 605 002
Website: http://sabda.sriaurobindoashram.org
Printed at Sri Aurobindo Ashram Press, Pondicherry
PRINTED IN INDIA

Publisher's Note

Prayers and Meditations consists of extracts from the Mother's spiritual diaries. Most of them are from the period 1912 to 1917. The 313 prayers reproduced here were selected by the Mother for publication. Written in French, they appear here in English translation.

A small collection of prayers — about one-fifth of the total — was brought out in English in 1941. Sri Aurobindo translated some of those prayers himself and, in the other cases, revised translations made by disciples. These prayers wholly or partly translated by Sri Aurobindo are marked in this volume with an asterisk (*).

Details about publication are provided in the Note on the Text.

Some give their soul to the Divine, some their life, some offer their work, some their money. A few consecrate all of themselves and all they have - soul, life, work, wealth; these are the true children of God. Others give nothing. these whatever their position, power and riches are for the Divine purpose valueless cyphers.

This book is meant for those who aspire for an utter consecration to the Divine

1941 - 1943.

This book comprises extracts from a diary written during years of intensive yogic discipline. It may serve as a spiritual guide to three principal categories of seekers: those who have undertaken self-mastery, those who want to find the road leading to the Divine, those who aspire to consecrate themselves more and more to the Divine Work.

The Mother

The Mother in Algeria, 1906-1907

November 2, 1912 *

ALTHOUGH my whole being is in theory consecrated to Thee, O Sublime Master, who art the life, the light and the love in all things, I still find it hard to carry out this consecration in detail. It has taken me several weeks to learn that the reason for this written meditation, its justification, lies in the very fact of addressing it daily to Thee. In this way I shall put into material shape each day a little of the conversation I have so often with Thee; I shall make my confession to Thee as well as it may be; not because I think I can tell Thee anything — for Thou art Thyself everything, but our artificial and exterior way of seeing and understanding is, if it may be so said, foreign to Thee, opposed to Thy nature. Still by turning towards Thee, by immersing myself in Thy light at the moment when I consider these things, little by little I shall see them more like what they really are, — until the day when, having made myself one in identity with Thee, I shall no more have anything to say to Thee, for then I shall be Thou. This is the goal that I would reach; towards this victory all my efforts will tend more and more. I aspire for the day when I can no longer say "I", for I shall be *Thou*.

How many times a day, still, I act without my action being consecrated to Thee; I at once become aware of it by an indefinable uneasiness which is translated in the sensibility of my body by a pang in my heart. I then make my action objective to myself and it seems to me ridiculous, childish or blameworthy; I deplore it, for a moment I am

1

sad, until I dive into Thee and, there losing myself with a child's confidence, await from Thee the inspiration and strength needed to set right the error in me and around me, — two things that are one; for I have now a constant and precise perception of the universal unity determining an absolute interdependence of all actions.

November 3, 1912*

LET Thy Light be in me like a Fire that makes all alive;
let Thy divine Love penetrate me. I aspire with all my
being for Thy reign as sovereign and master of my mind
and heart and body; let them be Thy docile instruments
and Thy faithful servitors.

3

November 19, 1912 *

I SAID yesterday to that young Englishman who is seeking for Thee with so sincere a desire, that I had definitively found Thee, that the Union was constant. Such is indeed the state of which I am conscious. All my thoughts go towards Thee, all my acts are consecrated to Thee; Thy Presence is for me an absolute, immutable, invariable fact, and Thy Peace dwells constantly in my heart. Yet I know that this state of union is poor and precarious compared with that which it will become possible for me to realise tomorrow, and I am as yet far, no doubt very far, from that identification in which I shall totally lose the notion of the "I", of that "I", which I still use in order to express myself, but which is each time a constraint, like a term unfit to express the thought that is seeking for expression. It seems to me indispensable for human communication, but all depends on what this "I" manifests; and how many times already, when I pronounce it, it is Thou who speakest in me, for I have lost the sense of separativity.

But all this is still in embryo and will continue to grow towards perfection. What an appeasing assurance there is in this serene confidence in Thy All-Might!

Thou art all, everywhere, and in all, and this body which acts is Thy own body, just as is the visible universe in its entirety; it is Thou who breathest, thinkest and lovest in this substance which, being Thyself, desires to be Thy willing servant.

November 26, 1912 *

WHAT a hymn of thanksgiving should I not be raising at each moment unto Thee! Everywhere and in everything around me Thou revealest Thyself and in me Thy Will and Consciousness express themselves always more and more clearly even to the point of my having almost entirely lost the gross illusion of "me" and "mine". If a few shadows, a few flaws can be seen in the great Light which manifests Thee, how shall they bear for long the marvellous brightness of Thy resplendent Love? This morning, the consciousness that I had of the way Thou art fashioning this being which was "I" can be roughly represented by a great diamond cut with regular geometrical facets, a diamond in its cohesion, firmness, pure limpidity, transparency, but a brilliant and radiant flame in its intense ever-progressive life. But it was something more, something better than all that, for nearly all sensation inner and outer was exceeded and that image only presented itself to my mind as I returned to conscious contact with the outer world.

It is Thou that makest the experience fertile, Thou who renderest life progressive, Thou who compellest the darkness to vanish in an instant before the Light, Thou who givest to Love all its power, Thou who everywhere raisest up matter in this ardent and wonderful aspiration, in this sublime thirst for Eternity.

Thou everywhere and always; nothing but *Thou* in the essence and in the manifestation.

O Shadow and Illusion, dissolve! O Suffering, fade and disappear! Lord Supreme, art Thou not there?

5

November 28, 1912 *

T HE outer life, the activity of each day and each instant, is it not the indispensable complement of our hours of meditation and contemplation? And is not the proportion of time given to each the exact image of the proportion which exists between the amount of effort to be made for the preparation and realisation? For meditation, contemplation, Union is the result obtained — the flower that blooms; the daily activity is the anvil on which all the elements must pass and repass in order to be purified, refined, made supple and ripe for the illumination which contemplation gives to them. All these elements must be thus passed one after the other through the crucible before outer activity becomes needless for the integral development. Then is this activity turned into the means to manifest Thee so as to awaken the other centers of consciousness to the same dual work of the forge and the illumination. Therefore are pride and satisfaction with oneself the worst of all obstacles. Very modestly we must take advantage of all the minute opportunities offered to knead and purify some of the innumerable elements, to make them supple, to make them impersonal, to teach them forgetfulness of self and abnegation and devotion and kindness and gentleness; and when all these modes of being have become habitual to them, then are they ready to participate in the Contemplation, and to identify themselves with Thee in the supreme Concentration. That is why it seems to me that the work must be long and slow even for the best and that striking conversions cannot be integral. They change the orientation of the being, they put it definitively on the straight path; but truly to attain the goal none can escape the need of innumerable experiences of every kind and every instant.

. . . O Supreme Master who shinest in my being and each thing, let Thy Light be manifest and the reign of Thy Peace come for all.

December 2, 1912 *

SO long as one element of the being, one movement of the thought is still subjected to outside influences, not solely under Thine, it cannot be said that the true Union is realised; there is still the horrible mixture without order and light, — for that element, that movement is a world, a world of disorder and darkness, as is the entire earth in the material world, as is the material world in the entire universe.

December 3, 1912 *

LAST night I had the experience of the effectivity of confident surrender to Thy guidance; when it is needful that something should be known, one knows it, and the more passive the mind to Thy illumination, the clearer and the more adequate is its expression.

I listened to Thee as Thou spokest in me, and I would have liked to write down what Thou saidst so that the formula in all its precision might not be lost, — for now I should not be able to repeat what was said. Then I thought that this care for conservation was again an insulting lack of confidence towards Thee, for Thou canst make of me all that I need to be, and in the measure in which my attitude allows Thee to act on me and in me, Thy omnipotence has no limits. To know that at each instant what must be surely is, as perfectly as is possible, for all those who know how to see Thee in everything and everywhere! No more fear, no more uneasiness, no more anguish; nothing but a perfect Serenity, an absolute Confidence, a supreme unwavering Peace.

December 5, 1912*

IN Peace and Silence the Eternal manifests; allow nothing to disturb you and the Eternal will manifest; have perfect equality in face of all and the Eternal will be there. . . . Yes, we should not put too much intensity, too much effort into our seeking for Thee; the effort and intensity become a veil in front of Thee; we must not desire to see Thee, for that is still a mental agitation which obscures Thy Eternal Presence; it is in the most complete Peace, Serenity and Equality that all is Thou even as Thou art all, and the least vibration in this perfectly pure and calm atmosphere is an obstacle to Thy manifestation. No haste, no inquietude, no tension, Thou, nothing but Thou, without any analysis or any objectivising, and Thou art there without a possible doubt, for all becomes a Holy Peace and a Sacred Silence.

And that is better than all the meditations in the world.

December 7, 1912*

LIKE a flame that burns in silence, like a perfume that rises straight upward without wavering, my love goes to Thee; and like the child who does not reason and has no care, I trust myself to Thee that Thy Will may be done, that Thy Light may manifest, Thy Peace radiate, Thy Love cover the world. When Thou willest I shall be in Thee, Thyself, and there shall be no more any distinction; I await that blessed hour without impatience of any kind, letting myself flow irresistibly toward it as a peaceful stream flows toward the boundless ocean.

Thy Peace is in me, and in that Peace I see Thee alone present in everything, with the calm of Eternity.

December 10, 1912*

O SUPREME Master, Eternal Teacher, it has been once more granted me to verify the unequalled effectivity of a full confidence in Thy leading. Thy Light was manifested through my mouth yesterday and it met no resistance in me; the instrument was willing, supple, keen of edge.

It is Thou who art the doer in each thing and each being, and he who is near enough to Thee to see Thee in all actions without exception, will know how to transform each act into a benediction.

To abide always in Thee is the one thing that matters, always and ever more and more in Thee, beyond illusions and the deceptions of the senses, not drawing back from action, refusing it, rejecting it — a struggle useless and pernicious — but living Thee alone in the act whatever it may be, ever and always Thee; then the illusion is dispelled, the falsehoods of the senses vanish, the bond of consequences is broken, all is transformed into a manifestation of the glory of Thy Eternal Presence.

So let it be. Amen.

December 11, 1912*

I AWAIT, without haste, without inquietude, the tearing of another veil, the Union made more complete. I know that the veil is formed of a whole mass of small imperfections, of attachments without number. . . . How shall all these disappear? Slowly, as the result of countless small efforts and a vigilance not faltering even for a moment, or suddenly, through a great illumination of Thy All-Puissant Love? I know not, I do not even put to myself the question; I wait, keeping watch as best I can, in the certitude that nothing exists save Thy Will, that Thou alone art the doer and I am the instrument; and when the instrument is ready for a completer manifestation, the manifestation will quite naturally take place.

Already there is heard from behind the veil the wordless symphony of gladness that reveals Thy sublime Presence.

February 5, 1913 *

THY voice is heard as a melodious chant in the stillness of my heart, and is translated in my head by words
which are inadequate and yet replete with Thee. And
these words are addressed to the Earth and say to her:
— Poor sorrowful Earth, remember that I am present in
thee and lose not hope; each effort, each grief, each joy
and each pang, each call of thy heart, each aspiration
of thy soul, each renewal of thy seasons, all, all without
exception, what seems to thee sorrowful and what seems
to thee joyous, what seems to thee ugly and what seems
to thee beautiful, all infallibly lead thee towards me, who
am endless Peace, shadowless Light, perfect Harmony,
Certitude, Rest and Supreme Blessedness.

Hearken, O Earth, to the sublime voice that arises,
Hearken and take new courage!

February 8, 1913 *

O LORD, Thou art my refuge and my blessing, my strength, my health, my hope, and my courage. Thou art supreme Peace, unalloyed Joy, perfect Serenity. My whole being prostrates before Thee in a gratitude beyond measure and a ceaseless worship; and that worship goes up from my heart and my mind towards Thee like the pure smoke of incense of the perfumes of India.

Let me be Thy herald among men, so that all who are ready may taste the beatitude that Thou grantest me in Thy infinite Mercy, and let Thy Peace reign upon earth.

February 10, 1913*

MY being goes up to Thee in thanksgiving, not because Thou usest this weak and imperfect body to manifest Thyself, but because *Thou dost manifest Thyself*, and that is the Splendour of splendours, the Joy of joys, the Marvel of marvels. All who seek Thee with ardour should understand that Thou art there whenever there is need of Thee; and if they could have the supreme faith to give up seeking Thee, but rather to await Thee, at each moment putting themselves integrally at Thy service, Thou wouldst be there whenever there was need of Thee; and is there not always need of Thee with us, whatever may be the different, and often unexpected, forms of Thy manifestation?

Let Thy glory be proclaimed,
And sanctify life;
Let it transform men's hearts,
And Thy Peace reign on earth.

February 12, 1913 *

As soon as all effort disappears from a manifestation, it becomes very simple, with the simplicity of a flower opening, manifesting its beauty and spreading its fragrance without clamour or vehement gesture. And in this simplicity lies the greatest power, the power which is least mixed and least gives rise to harmful reactions. The power of the vital should be mistrusted, it is a tempter on the path of the work, and there is always a risk of falling into its trap, for it gives you the taste of immediate results; and, in our first eagerness to do the work well, we let ourselves be carried away to make use of this power. But very soon it deflects all our action from the right course and introduces a seed of illusion and death into what we do.

Simplicity, simplicity! How sweet is the purity of Thy Presence! . . .

March 13, 1913 *

... LET the pure perfume of sanctification burn always, rising higher and higher, and straighter and straighter, like the ceaseless prayer of the integral being, desiring to unite with Thee so as to manifest Thee.

May 11, 1913*

As soon as I have no longer any material responsibilities, all thoughts about these things flee far away from me, and I am solely and entirely occupied with Thee and Thy service. Then, in that perfect peace and serenity, I unite my will to Thine, and in that integral silence I listen to Thy truth and hear its expression. It is by becoming conscious of Thy Will and identifying ours with Thine that there is found the secret of true liberty and all-puissance, the secret of the regeneration of forces and the transfiguration of the being.

To be constantly and integrally at one with Thee is to have the assurance that we shall overcome every obstacle and triumph over all difficulties, both within and without.

O Lord, Lord, a boundless joy fills my heart, songs of gladness surge through my head in marvellous waves, and in the full confidence of Thy certain triumph I find a sovereign Peace and an invincible Power. Thou fillest my being, Thou animatest it, Thou settest in motion its hidden springs, Thou illuminest its understanding, Thou intensifiest its life, Thou increasest tenfold its love; and I no longer know whether the universe is I or I the universe, whether Thou art in me or I in Thee; Thou alone art and all is Thou; and the streams of Thy infinite grace fill and overflow the world.

Sing O lands, sing O peoples, sing O men,
The Divine Harmony is there.

June 15, 1913

EVEN he who might have attained a perfect contemplation in silence and solitude would have arrived at it only by withdrawing from his body, by disregarding it; and so the substance of which the body is constituted would remain as impure, as imperfect as before, since he would have left it to itself; and by a misguided mysticism, through the lure of supraphysical splendours, the egoistic desire to unite with Thee for his own personal satisfaction, he would have turned his back upon the very reason of his earthly existence, he would have refused like a coward to accomplish his mission — the redemption and purification of Matter. To know that a part of our being is perfectly pure, to commune with this purity, to be identified with it, can be useful only if this knowledge is later used to hasten the transfiguration of the earth, to accomplish Thy sublime work.

June 17, 1913

GRANT, O Lord, that I may be like a fire that illumines and gives warmth, like a spring of water that quenches thirst, like a tree that shelters and protects. . . . Men are so unhappy and ignorant and have so great a need of help.

My trust in Thee, the certitude within me grow deeper day by day; and day by day too I feel Thy love more ardent within my heart, Thy light more brilliant and yet also more sweet; and more and more am I unable to distinguish Thy Work from my life and my individual being from the entire earth.

O Lord, Lord, Thy Splendour is infinite, marvellous is Thy Truth; and Thy all-powerful Love shall save the world.

June 18, 1913 *

To turn towards Thee, unite with Thee, live in Thee and for Thee, is supreme happiness, unmixed joy, immutable peace; it is to breathe infinity, to soar in eternity, no longer feel one's limits, escape from time and space. Why do men flee from these boons as though they feared them? What a strange thing is ignorance, that source of all suffering! How miserable that obscurity which keeps men away from the very thing which would bring them happiness and subjects them to this painful school of ordinary existence fashioned entirely from struggle and suffering!

June 27, 1913

T HY voice is so modest, so impartial, so sublime in
its patience and mercy that it does not make itself heard
with any authority, any force of will but comes like a
cool breeze, sweet and pure, like a crystalline murmur
that brings a note of harmony to a discordant concert.
Yet, for him who knows how to listen to the note, to
breathe that breeze, it holds such treasures of beauty,
such a fragrance of pure serenity and noble grandeur,
that all foolish illusions vanish or are transformed into a
joyful acceptance of the marvellous truth that has been
glimpsed.

July 21, 1913 *

. . . **Y**ET what patience is needed! How imperceptible the stages of progress! . . .

Oh! how I call Thee from the very depths of my heart, True Light, Sublime Love, Divine Master who art the source of our light and of our living, our guide and our protector, the Soul of our soul and the Life of our life, the Reason of our being, the supreme Knowledge, the immutable Peace!

July 23, 1913

O LORD, inconceivable Splendour, may Thy Beauty spread through all the earth, may Thy Love be kindled in every heart and Thy Peace reign over all.

A deep and solemn chant, smiling and subtle, rises from my heart, and I do not know whether this chant goes from me to Thee or comes from Thee to me or whether Thou and I and the entire universe are this marvellous chant of which I have just become conscious. . . . Surely there is no longer any Thou or I or any separate universe; only an immense harmony is there, sublime and infinite, which is all things and of which all things will one day grow aware. It is the harmony of boundless Love, Love victorious over all suffering and all obscurity.

By this law of Love, Thy law, I want to live more and more integrally; to it unreservedly I give myself.

And all my being exults in an inexpressible Peace.

August 2, 1913

THIS morning, as I was glancing over the month that is beginning and wondering how I could serve Thee better, I heard the small voice within like a murmur in the silence, and this is what it said to me: "See how very little all outer circumstances matter. Why strive and strain so to realise thy own conception of Truth? Be more supple, more trusting. The only duty is not to let oneself be troubled by anything. To torment oneself about doing the right thing causes as much harm as a bad will. Only in a calm as of deep waters can be found the possibility of True Service."

And this reply was so luminous and pure, it carried within itself such a striking reality, that the state it described was communicated without any difficulty. It seemed to me I was floating in the calm of deep waters; I understood; I saw clearly what the best attitude would be; and now I have only to ask Thee, O Sublime Master, my Supreme Teacher, to give me the strength and clear-sightedness I need to remain constantly in this state.

"Do not torment thyself, child. Silence, peace, peace."

August 8, 1913

O SWEET harmony that dwellest in all things, sweet harmony that fillest my heart, manifest thyself in the most external forms of life, in every feeling, every thought, every action.

All is to me beautiful, harmonious, silent, despite the outer turmoil. And in this silence it is Thou, O Lord, whom I see; and I see Thee in so unique a way that I can express this perception only as that of an unvarying smile. In truth, the real nature of the feeling experienced in the presence of the sweetest, most calm, most compassionate smile has a poor resemblance to what I feel when I see Thee in this way.

May Thy Peace be with all.

August 15, 1913

IN this even-fall, Thy Peace deepens and grows more sweet and Thy Voice more clear and distinct in the silence that fills my being.

O Divine Master, Thine is all our life, our thought, our love, all our being. Take unto Thyself once more what is Thine; for Thou art ourselves in our Reality.

August 16, 1913

O LOVE, divine Love, Thou fillest my whole being and overflowest on every side. I am Thyself even as Thou art I, and I see Thee in each being, each thing, from the soft breath of the passing breeze to the glorious sun which gives us light and is a symbol of Thee.

O Thou whom I cannot understand, in the silence of the purest devotion I adore Thee.

August 17, 1913

O LORD, Master of our life, let us soar very high above all care for our material preservation. Nothing is more humiliating and depressing than these thoughts so constantly turned towards the preservation of the body, these preoccupations with health, the means of subsistence, the framework of life. . . . How very insignificant is all this, a thin smoke that a simple breath can disperse or a single thought turned towards Thee dispel like a vain mirage!

Deliver those who are in this bondage, O Lord, even as those who are the slaves of passion. On the path that leads to Thee these obstacles are at once terrible and puerile — terrible for those who are yet under their sway, puerile for one who has passed beyond.

How shall I describe that utter relief, that delightful lightness which comes when one is free from all anxiety for oneself, for one's life and health and satisfaction, and even one's progress?

This relief, this deliverance Thou hast granted to me, O Thou, Divine Master, Life of my life and Light of my light, O Thou who unceasingly teachest me love and makest me know the purpose of my existence.

It is Thou who livest in me, Thou alone; and why should I be preoccupied with myself and what might happen to me? Without Thee the dust constituting this body that strives to manifest Thee, would disperse amorphous and inconscient; without Thee this sensibility which makes possible a relation with all other centres of

30

manifestation, would vanish into a dark inertia; without Thee this thought that animates and illumines the whole being, would be vague, vacant, unrealised; without Thee the sublime love which vivifies, coordinates, animates and gives warmth to all things would be a yet unawakened possibility. Without Thee all is inert, brute or inconscient. Thou art all that illumines and enraptures us, the whole reason of our existence and all our goal. Is this not enough to cure us of every personal thought, to make us spread our wings and soar above the contingencies of material life, so as to fly away into Thy divine atmosphere and be able to return as Thy messengers to the earth to announce the glorious tidings of Thy approaching Advent?

O Divine Master, sublime Friend, marvellous Teacher, in a fecund silence I bow to Thee.

October 7, 1913

THIS return after an absence of three months to the house which is consecrated to Thee, O Lord, has been the occasion of two experiences. The first is that in my outer being, my surface consciousness, I no longer have the least feeling of being in my own home and the owner of anything there: I am a stranger in a strange land, much more of a stranger here than in the open countryside among the trees; and I smile, now that I have learnt what I did not know, I smile at the idea of having felt myself "mistress of the house", an idea I had before my departure; it was necessary for all pride to be broken, crushed, trampled down definitively so that I could at last understand, see and feel things as they are. I used to offer to Thee this dwelling, O Lord, as though it were possible that I should possess something and consequently be able to make an offering of it to Thee. All is Thine, O Lord, it is Thou who placest all things at our disposal; but how blind we are when we imagine that we can be owners of any one of these! I am a visitor here as elsewhere, as everywhere, Thy messenger and Thy servant upon earth, a stranger among men, and yet the very soul of their life, the love of their heart. . . .

Secondly, the whole atmosphere of the house is charged with a religious solemnity; one immediately goes down into the depths; the meditations here are more in-gathered and serious; dispersion vanishes to give place to concentration; and I feel this concentration literally descending from my head and entering into my heart;

32

and the heart seems to attain a depth more profound than the head. It is as though for three months I had been loving with my head and that now I were beginning to love with my heart; and this brings me an incomparable solemnity and sweetness of feeling.

A new door has opened in my being and an immensity has appeared before me.

I cross the threshold with devotion, feeling hardly worthy yet of entering upon this hidden path, veiled to the sight and as though invisibly luminous within.

All is changed, all is new; the old wrappings have fallen off and the new-born child half-opens its eyes to the shining dawn.

November 22, 1913

A FEW minutes passed in silence before Thee are worth centuries of felicity. . . .

Grant, O Lord, that all shadows may be dispelled and that I may be more and more Thy faithful servant in constancy and serenity. Before Thee may my heart be pure as a pure crystal, so that wholly it may reflect Thee.

Oh! the sweetness of abiding in silence before Thee....

November 25, 1913

THE greatest enemy of a silent contemplation turned towards Thee is surely this constant subconscient registering of the multitude of phenomena with which we come into contact. So long as we are mentally active, our conscious thought veils for us this overactivity of our subconscious receptivity; an entire part of our sensibility, and perhaps not the smallest, acts like a cine-camera without our knowledge and indeed to our detriment. It is only when we silence our active thought, which is relatively easy, that we see this multitude of little subconscious notations surging up from every side and often drowning us under their overwhelming flood. So it happens that, as soon as we attempt to enter the silence of deep contemplation, we are assailed by countless thoughts — if thoughts they could be called — which do not interest us in the least, do not represent for us any active desire, any conscious attachment, but only prove to us our inability to control what may be described as the mechanical receptivity of our subconscient. A considerable labour is needed to silence all these useless noises, to stop this wearisome train of images and to purify one's mind of these thousand little nothings, so obstructing and worthless. And it is so much time uselessly lost; it is a terrible wastage.

And the remedy? In an over-simple way, certain ascetic disciplines recommend solitude and inaction: sheltering one's subconscient from all possible registration; that seems to me a childish remedy, for it leaves the ascetic

35

at the mercy of the first surprise-attack; and if one day, confident of being perfectly master of himself, he wants to come back among his fellowmen in order to help them, his subconscient, so long deprived of its activity of reception, will surely indulge it more intensively than ever before, as soon as the least opportunity offers.

There is certainly another remedy. What is it? Undoubtedly, one must learn to control one's subconscient just as one controls one's conscious thought. There must be many ways of achieving this. Regular introspection in the Buddhist manner and a methodical analysis of one's dreams — formed almost always from this subconscious registration — are part of the method to be found. But there is surely something more rapidly effective. . . .

O Lord, Eternal Master, Thou shalt be the Teacher, the Inspirer; Thou wilt teach me what should be done, so that after an indispensable application of it to myself, I may make others also benefit from what Thou hast taught me.

With a loving and trustful devotion, I bow to Thee.

November 28, 1913

IN this calm concentration which comes before day-
break, more than at any other moment, my thought rises
to Thee, O Lord of our being, in an ardent prayer.

Grant that this day which is about to dawn may bring
to the earth and to men a little more of pure light and true
peace; may Thy manifestation be more complete and Thy
sweet law more widely recognised; may something higher,
nobler, more true be revealed to mankind; may a vaster
and deeper love spread abroad so that all painful wounds
may be healed; and may this first sunbeam dawning upon
the earth be the herald of joy and harmony, a symbol of
the glorious splendour hidden in the essence of life.

*O Divine Master, grant that today may bring to us
a completer consecration to Thy Will, a more integral
gift of ourselves to Thy work, a more total forgetfulness
of self, a greater illumination, a purer love. Grant that
in a communion growing ever deeper, more constant and
entire, we may be united always more and more closely to
Thee and become Thy servitors worthy of Thee. Remove
from us all egoism, root out all petty vanity, greed and
obscurity. May we be all ablaze with Thy divine Love;
make us Thy torches in the world.*

A silent hymn of praise rises from my heart like the
white smoke of incense of the perfumes of the East.

And in the serenity of a perfect surrender, I bow to
Thee in the light of the rising day.

November 29, 1913

WHY all this noise, all this movement, this vain and futile agitation; why this whirlwind carrying men away like a swarm of flies caught in a storm? How sad is the sight of all that wasted energy, all those useless efforts! When will they stop dancing like puppets on a string, pulled they know not by whom or what? When will they find time to sit quietly and go within, to recollect themselves and open that inner door which screens from them Thy priceless treasures, Thy infinite boons? . . .

How sorrowful and miserable seems to me their life of ignorance and obscurity, their life of mad agitation and unprofitable dispersion! — when one single spark of Thy sublime light, one single drop of Thy divine love, can transform this suffering into an ocean of delight!

O Lord, my prayer soars towards Thee: May they know at last Thy peace and that calm and irresistible strength which comes of an immutable serenity — the privilege of those whose eyes have been opened and who are able to contemplate Thee in the flaming core of their being.

But the hour of Thy manifestation is come.

And soon hymns of gladness will burst forth on every side.

Before the solemnity of this hour I bow down in devotion.

December 13, 1913

GIVE me Thy light, O Lord, grant that I do not fall into any error. Grant that the infinite reverence, the utter devotion, that intense and profound love I bring to Thee may be radiant, convincing, contagious, and be awakened in every heart.

O Lord, Eternal Master, Thou art my Light and my Peace; guide my steps, open my eyes, illumine my heart, and lead me on the paths that go straight to Thee.

O Lord, Lord, grant that I may have no other will than Thine and that all my acts may be an expression of Thy divine law.

A great Light floods my whole being, and I am no longer conscious of anything but Thee. . . .

Peace, peace, peace upon all the earth.

December 16, 1913

PURE and disinterested love, Thy love in what we are able to perceive and manifest of it, is the sole key that can open all hearts that seek for Thee. Those who follow the path of the intellect may have a very high and true conception; they may have all the information about the true life, the life One with Thee, but they do not *know* it; they have no inner experience of that life and are ignorant of all contact with Thee. These men whose knowledge is intellectual and whose action is confined to a construction which they believe to be the best, are the most difficult of all to convert; it is harder to awaken the consciousness of the Divine in them than in any other person of goodwill. Love alone can work this miracle, for love opens all doors, penetrates every wall, clears every obstacle. And a little true love does more than the most beautiful speeches.

Lord, let this pure flower of love blossom in me, that it may give its fragrance to all those who come near us, and that this fragrance may sanctify them.

In this love lie peace and joy, the fount of all strength and all realisation. It is the infallible healer, the supreme consoler; it is the victor, the sovereign teacher.

O Lord, my sweet Master, Thou whom I adore in silence and to whom I have entirely consecrated myself, Thou who governest my life, kindle in my heart the flame of Thy pure love that it may burn like a glowing brazier, consuming all imperfections and transforming into a comforting warmth and radiating light the dead wood of egoism and the black coals of ignorance.

O Lord, I turn towards Thee with a devotion at once joyful and solemn and I implore Thee:
Let Thy love manifest,
Thy reign come.
May Thy peace govern the world.

December 29, 1913

O LORD, grant that this collective convention of the ending year be for us also the occasion to put an end to a whole lot of bonds and attachments, illusions and weaknesses which have no longer any purpose in our lives. At every moment we must shake off the past like falling dust, that it may not soil the virgin path which, at every moment also, is opening before us.

May our mistakes, acknowledged and rectified within us, be no more than vain mirages powerless to bring any consequences and, pressing our foot down firmly upon all that no longer should exist, on all ignorance, all obscurity, all egoism, may we take our flight boldly towards wider horizons and intenser light, a more perfect compassion, a more disinterested love. . . . towards Thee.

I hail Thee, O Lord, Master of our life, and I want to proclaim Thy reign over all the earth.

January 1, 1914

T O Thee, supreme Dispenser of all boons, to Thee who givest life its justification, by making it pure, beautiful and good, to Thee, Master of our destinies and goal of all our aspirations, was consecrated the first minute of this new year.

May it be completely glorified by this consecration; may those who hope for Thee, seek Thee in the right path; may those who seek Thee find Thee, and those who suffer, not knowing where the remedy lies, feel Thy life gradually piercing the hard crust of their obscure consciousness.

I bow down in deep devotion and in boundless gratitude before Thy beneficent splendour; in the name of the earth I give Thee thanks for manifesting Thyself; in its name I implore Thee to manifest Thyself ever more fully, in an uninterrupted growth of Light and Love.

Be the sovereign Master of our thoughts, our feelings, our actions.

Thou art our reality, the only Reality.

Without Thee all is falsehood and illusion, all is dismal obscurity.

In Thee are life and light and joy.

In Thee is supreme Peace.

January 2, 1914

THIS marvellous silence manifests Thee despite the mad human agitation — the immutable and constant silence so living in all things that one has but to listen to hear it, in contrast with all that is futile noise, vain agitation, useless dispersion of energies. Let it flower in our being as a source of light and peace; may its power radiate over all in beneficent streams.

Thou art the savour of all life and the reason for all activity, the goal of our thoughts.

44

January 3, 1914

IT is always good to look within oneself from time to time and see that one is nothing and can do nothing, but afterwards one must turn one's eyes to Thee, knowing that Thou art all and Thou canst do all.

Thou art the life of our life
and the light of our being,
Thou art the master of our destinies.

January 4, 1914

THE tide of materialistic thoughts is always on the watch, waiting for the least weakness, and if we relax but one moment from our vigilance, if we are even slightly negligent, it rushes in and invades us from all sides, submerging under its heavy flood the result sometimes of numberless efforts. Then the being enters a sort of torpor, its physical needs of food and sleep increase, its intelligence is clouded, its inner vision veiled, and in spite of the little interest it really finds in such superficial activities, they occupy it almost exclusively. This state is extremely painful and tiring, for nothing is more tiring than materialistic thoughts, and the mind, worn out, suffers like a caged bird which cannot spread its wings and yet longs to be able to soar freely.

But perhaps this state has its own use which I do not see. . . . In any case, I do not struggle; and like a child in its mother's arms, like a fervent disciple at the feet of his master, I trust myself to Thee and surrender to Thy guidance, sure of Thy victory.

January 5, 1914

FOR a long while I have been sitting with this note-book before me, unable to make up my mind to write, so much is all within me mediocre, worthless, insipid, hope-lessly commonplace. Not a single thought in my head, not a single feeling in my heart, a complete indifference to everything and an insurmountable dullness.

How can such a state be of any use?

I am a veritable zero in the world.

But all this is not at all important. And provided Thy work is accomplished, Thy manifestation takes place and the earth becomes more and more Thy harmonious and fruitful kingdom, it matters little whether I accomplish this Work or not.

And as it is certain that It will be done, I should have no reason to worry even if I felt like it. From the depths to the outermost surface, all this, my being, is only a handful of dust; it is but natural that it should be scattered on the winds and leave no trace behind. . . .

January 6, 1914

THOU art the one and only goal of my life and the centre of my aspiration, the pivot of my thought, the key of the synthesis of my being. And as Thou art beyond all sensation, all feeling and all thought, Thou art the living but ineffable experience, the Reality lived in the depths of the being but untranslatable in our poor words; and it is because human intelligence is powerless to reduce Thee to a formula that some, a little disdainfully, label "sentiment" the knowledge that it is possible to have of Thee, but it is surely as far from sentiment as it is from thought. So long as one has not attained this supreme Knowledge, one has no solid basis or lasting centre for one's mental and emotional synthesis, and all other intellectual constructions can only be arbitrary, artificial and vain.

Thou art eternal silence and perfect peace in what we are able to perceive of Thee.

Thou art all the perfection we must acquire, all the marvels to be realised, all the splendour to be manifested.

And all our words are but children's babblings when we venture to speak of Thee.

In silence is the greatest reverence.

January 7, 1914

GIVE them all, O Lord, Thy peace and light, open their blinded eyes and their darkened understanding; calm their futile worries and their vain anxieties. Turn their gaze away from themselves and give them the joy of being consecrated to Thy work without calculation or mental reservation. Let Thy beauty flower in all things, awaken Thy love in all hearts, so that Thy eternally progressive order may be realised upon earth and Thy harmony be spread until the day all becomes Thyself in perfect purity and peace.

Oh! let all tears be wiped away, all suffering relieved, all anguish dispelled, and let calm serenity dwell in every heart and powerful certitude strengthen every mind. Let Thy life flow through all like a regenerating stream that all may turn to Thee and draw from that contemplation the energy for all victories.

January 8, 1914

LET us shun the paths that are too easy and ask no effort, the paths which give us the illusion of having reached our goal; let us shun that negligence which opens the door to every downfall, that complacent self-admiration which leads to every abyss. Let us understand that however great may have been our efforts, our struggles, even our victories, compared with the distance yet to be travelled, the one we have already covered is nothing; and that all are equal — infinitesimal grains of dust or identical stars — before Eternity.

But Thou art the conqueror of all obstacles, the Light that illumines all ignorance, the Love that vanquishes all pride. And no error can persist in front of Thee.

January 9, 1914

LORD, incomprehensible reality, Thou who ever fleest
before our conquest, effective though it may be, Thou
who shalt always be the Unknown despite all that we
shall learn to know of Thee, despite all that we shall
ravish from Thy eternal mystery, we would go forward,
making a complete and constant effort, combining all the
multiple paths leading to Thee, go forward like a rising,
indomitable tide, breaking down all obstacles, crossing
every barrier, lifting up every veil, scattering all clouds,
piercing through all darkness, go forward towards Thee,
ever to Thee, in a movement so powerful, so irresistible
that a whole multitude may be drawn in our wake, and
the earth, conscious of Thy new and eternal Presence, understand at last its true purpose, and live in the harmony
and peace of Thy sovereign realisation.

Teach us always more,
Give us more light,
Dispel our ignorance,
Illumine our minds,
Transfigure our hearts,
And give us the Love that never runs dry, and makes
Thy sweet law flower in every being.
We are Thine for all Eternity.

January 10, 1914

My aspiration rises towards Thee ever the same in its almost childlike form, so ordinary in its simplicity, but my call is ever more ardent, and behind the faltering words there is all the fervour of my concentrated will. And I implore Thee, O Lord, in spite of the naïveté of this expression that is hardly intellectual, I implore Thee for more true light, true purity, sincerity and love, and all this for all, for the multitude constituting what I call my being, and for the multitude constituting the universal being; I implore Thee, though I know that it is perfectly useless to implore Thee, for we alone, in our ignorance and ill-will, can stand in the way of Thy glorious and total manifestation, but something childlike within me finds a support in this mental attitude; I implore Thee that the peace of Thy reign may spread throughout the earth.

O inaccessible summit which we unceasingly scale without ever reaching Thee, sole Reality of our being whom we believe we have found only to see Thee immediately escape us, marvellous state which we think we have seized but which leads us farther and farther into ever unexplored depths and immensities; no one can say, "I have known Thee," and yet all carry Thee in themselves, and in the silence of their soul can hear the echo of Thy voice; but this silence is itself progressive, and whatever be the perfection of the union we have realised, as long as we belong by our body to the world of relativity, this Union with Thee can always grow more perfect.

But all these words we use to speak about Thee are only idle talk. Grant that I may become Thy faithful servitor.

January 11, 1914

EVERY moment all the unforeseen, the unexpected, the unknown is before us, every moment the universe is created anew in its entirety and in every one of its parts. And if we had a truly living faith, if we had the absolute certitude of Thy omnipotence and Thy sole reality, Thy manifestation could at each moment become so evident that the whole universe would be transformed by it. But we are so enslaved to everything that is around us and has gone before us, we are so influenced by the whole totality of manifested things, and our faith is so weak that we are yet unable to serve as intermediaries for the great miracle of transfiguration. . . . But, Lord, I know that it will come one day. I know that a day will come when Thou wilt transform all those who come to us; Thou wilt transform them so radically that, liberated completely from the bonds of the past, they will begin to live in Thee an entirely new life, a life made solely of Thee, with Thee as its sovereign Lord. And in this way all anxieties will be transformed into serenity, all anguish into peace, all doubts into certainties, all ugliness into harmony, all egoism into self-giving, all darkness into light and all suffering into immutable happiness.

But art Thou not already performing this beautiful miracle? I see it flowering everywhere around us!

O divine law of beauty and love, supreme liberator, there is no obstacle to Thy power. Only our own blindness deprives us of the comforting sight of Thy constant victory.

My heart sings a hymn of gladness and my thought is illumined with joy.

Thy transcendent and marvellous love is the sovereign Master of the world.

January 12, 1914

A TEACHING can be profitable only if it is perfectly sincere, that is, if it is lived while it is being given, and words often repeated, thoughts expressed frequently can no longer be sincere. . . .

January 13, 1914

THOU hast passed, O Lord, like a great wave of love over my life, and when I was immersed in it I knew integrally and intensely that I had offered to Thee — when? I do not know, at no precise moment and most probably always — my thought, my heart, my body in a living holocaust.

And in that great love which enveloped me and that consciousness of perfect renunciation there was an immense serenity vaster than the universe and a sweetness so intense and so full of infinite compassion that tears began to flow slowly from my eyes. Nothing could have been more remote from both suffering and happiness, it was unutterable peace.

O sublime Love, centre of our life, Marvel of marvels, at last I find Thee again and live anew in Thee, but how much more powerfully, how much more consciously than before! How much better I know Thee, understand Thee! Each time I find Thee anew, my communion with Thee grows more integral, more complete, more definitive.

O Presence of ineffable beauty, thought of supreme redemption, sovereign power of salvation, with what joy all my being feels Thee living within it, sole principle of its life and of all life, wonderful builder of all thought, all will, all consciousness. On this world of illusion, this sombre nightmare, Thou hast bestowed Thy divine reality, and each atom of matter contains something of Thy Absolute.

Thou art, Thou livest, Thou radiatest, Thou reignest.

January 19, 1914

O LORD, divine Master of Love, Thou art the eternal victor, and those who become perfectly attuned to Thee, those who live for Thee alone and by Thee alone, cannot but win all victories; for in Thee is the supreme force, the force of complete disinterestedness, of perfect clear-sightedness, sovereign kindness.

In Thee, by Thee, all is transfigured and glorified; in Thee is found the key to all mysteries and all powers. But one can attain Thee only if one no longer desires anything except to live in Thee, serve Thee, make Thy divine work triumph more swiftly for the salvation of a greater number of men.

O Lord, Thou alone art real and all else is an illusion; for when one lives in Thee one sees and understands all things, nothing escapes Thy perfect knowledge, but everything wears another appearance; for all is Thou in essence, all being the fruit of Thy work, of Thy magnanimous intervention; and in the most sinister darkness Thou couldst kindle a star.

May our devotion grow ever deeper.

May our consecration grow ever more perfect.

And mayst Thou, already the real sovereign of life, become in effect its true sovereign.

January 24, 1914*

O THOU who art the sole reality of our being, O sublime Master of love, Redeemer of life, let me have no longer any other consciousness than of Thee at every instant and in each being. When I do not live solely with Thy life, I agonise, I sink slowly towards extinction; for Thou art my only reason for existence, my one goal, my single support. I am like a timid bird not yet sure of its wings and hesitating to take its flight; let me soar to reach definitive identity with Thee.

January 29, 1914

IT is Thy Presence in every being, O divine Master of love, that makes it possible for every man, even the most cruel, to be open to pity and even the most vile to respect, almost despite himself, honour and justice. It is Thou who, beyond all conventions and prejudices, illuminest with a special light, divine and pure, all that we are and all that we do, and makest us see clearly the difference between what we actually are and what we could be.

Thou art the impassable barrier set up against the excess of evil, darkness and ill-will; Thou art the living hope in every heart of all possible and future perfections.

To Thee all the fervour of my adoration.

Thou art the gateway within reach of our conception leading to unsuspected and inconceivable splendours, splendours which will be revealed to us progressively.

January 30, 1914

ALL that is conscious within me belongs unreservedly to Thee, and gradually I shall strive always harder to conquer the subconscient, the yet dark bedrock.

O divine Master of love, eternal Teacher, Thou guidest our lives. It is in Thee alone and for Thee alone that we want to live; enlighten our consciousness, guide our steps, and grant that we may do the utmost we can, using all our energies solely to serve Thee.

61

January 31, 1914

EVERY morning may our thought rise fervently towards Thee, asking Thee how we can manifest and serve Thee best. At every moment in the manifold choices which we can make and which, despite their apparent insignificance, are always of great importance — since according to our decision we become subject to one category of determinisms or another — at every moment may our attitude be such that Thy divine Will may determine our choice and that thus it may be Thou who directest our entire life. According to the consciousness in which we are when taking a decision, we become subject to the determinism of the order of realities in which we are conscious; whence the consequences, often unforeseen and troublesome, that are contradictory to the general orientation of one's life and form obstacles which are sometimes terrible to overcome later. Therefore, O Lord, Divine Master of love, we want to be conscious of Thee and Thee alone, be identified with Thy supreme law each time we take a decision, each time we choose, so that it may be Thy Will which moves us, and that our life be thus effectively and integrally consecrated to Thee.

In Thy Light we shall see, in Thy Knowledge we shall know, in Thy Will we shall realise.

February 1, 1914 *

I TURN towards Thee who art everywhere and within all and outside all, intimate essence of all and remote from all, centre of condensation for all energies, creator of conscious individualities: I turn towards Thee and salute Thee, O liberator of the worlds, and, identified with Thy divine love, I contemplate the earth and its creatures, this mass of substance put into forms perpetually destroyed and renewed, this swarming mass of aggregates which are dissolved as soon as constituted, of beings who imagine that they are conscient and permanent individualities and who are as ephemeral as a breath, always alike or almost the same, in their diversity, repeating indefinitely the same desires, the same tendencies, the same appetites, the same ignorant errors.

But from time to time Thy sublime light shines in a being and radiates through him over the world, and then a little wisdom, a little knowledge, a little disinterested faith, heroism and compassion penetrates men's hearts, transforms their minds and sets free a few elements from that sorrowful and implacable wheel of existence to which their blind ignorance subjects them.

But how much greater a splendour than all that have gone before, how marvellous a glory and light would be needed to draw these beings out of the horrible aberration in which they are plunged by the life of cities and so-called civilisations! What a formidable and, at the same time, divinely sweet puissance would be needed to turn aside all these wills from the bitter struggle for their selfish,

63

mean and foolish satisfactions, to snatch them from this vortex which hides death behind its treacherous glitter, and turn them towards Thy conquering harmony!

O Lord, eternal Master, enlighten us, guide our steps, show us the way towards the realisation of Thy law, towards the accomplishment of Thy work.

I adore Thee in silence and listen to Thee in a religious concentration.

February 2, 1914

O LORD, I would like to be so ardent a love that all lonelinesses may be filled up by it and all sorrows soothed.

O Lord, I cry unto Thee: Make me a burning brazier which consumes all suffering and transforms it into joyous light irradiating the hearts of all! ....

Grant my prayer: Transform me into a brazier of pure love and boundless compassion.

February 5, 1914

WHAT could be said that is not always the very same aspiration: the law of divine love, the purest expression of what we can conceive of Thee, must be realised more and more upon earth and triumph over all ignorant egoism; we must become more and more perfectly the faithful servitors of that power of love and light, we must live in it, by it; that alone must live and act in us.

O Lord, become the sovereign Master of our lives and dispel all the obscurities which can still prevent us from seeing Thee and constantly communing with Thee.

Liberate us from all ignorance, liberate us from ourselves that we may open wide the doors of Thy glorious manifestation.

February 7, 1914

FOR him who, by being integrally united with Thee, is constantly conscious of what expresses Thee most perfectly in action considering the circumstances, no external rule is any longer necessary. The principles of life are in sum only makeshifts for diminishing as far as possible the ignorance of those who do not know Thee yet, and for counteracting somehow or other the moments of blindness and obscurity of those who have only an intermittent contact with Thee.

To make rules for oneself and to make them as general, that is, as supple as possible, is good, but provided one considers them only as artificial lights which should not be used except when the full natural light of communion with Thee fails. Besides, a constant revision of these rules is imperative, for they can be only the expression of a present knowledge and must necessarily gain by all growth and improvement of knowledge.

That is why when meditating upon the attitude one should have towards all those who come to us, in order not only to refrain from doing them any harm but, above all, to strive to do them the utmost possible good — that is, to help them as best one can in making the supreme discovery, the discovery of Thee within them — I saw clearly that no rule was vast and supple enough to be perfectly adapted to Thy law, and that the only true solution was to be always in communion with Thee, so that it could be adapted perfectly to all the infinite variety of circumstances.

67

February 8, 1914

O LORD, sweet Master of love, Thou who bringest us out of the darkness to awaken us to consciousness, who deliverest us from suffering to make us commune within Thy eternal peace, every morning my aspiration soars ardently towards Thee, and I implore that my being, integrally awake to Thy knowledge, may now live only by Thee, in Thee, for Thee; I implore that more and more perfectly identified with Thee, I may now be only Thyself manifested in word and act; I implore that all those who come to us, all who are in contact with us, may awaken to the full knowledge of Thy divine presence, Thy sovereign law, and let themselves be definitively transformed by it; I implore that all men upon earth, in spite of their bitter suffering, may feel dawning in it the sublime consolation of Thy light and love, and the marvellous comfort of Thy peace; I implore that every substance impregnated more and more by Thy sovereign forces may put up an ever-diminishing resistance of blind ignorance against Thee, and that triumphing over all darkness Thou mayst transfigure definitively and integrally this universe of strife and anguish into a universe of harmony and peace. . . .

So that Thy law may be fulfilled.

February 9, 1914

WHATEVER names may be given to Thee, O Lord, by the élite of humanity, athirst for something absolute, it seeks ardently for Thee. Even those who seem to move farthest away from Thee, even those who are exclusively occupied with themselves, are they not searching for an absolute in sensation, an absolute in satisfaction, and in spite of its vanity that search also can some day lead to Thee; Thou art far too much at the core, at the heart of all things for even the very worst egoisms not to be transformed by Thee into aspirations. . . . The only thing we must fear and avoid is the inertia of inconscience, of blind and heavy ignorance. That state lies at the very bottom of the infinite ladder that rises towards Thee. And all Thy effort consists in pulling Matter out of this primeval darkness so as to awaken it to consciousness. Even passion is preferable to inconscience. We must therefore go constantly forward to conquer that universal bedrock of inconscience and through our own organism transform it gradually into luminous consciousness.

O Lord, sweet Master of love, Thou whom I see so living, so conscious within all things, I adore Thee with a boundless devotion.

February 10, 1914

WITH peace in our hearts, with light in our minds, we feel Thee, O Lord, so living within us that we await events with serenity, knowing that Thy path is everywhere, since we carry it in our own being, and that in all circumstances we can become the heralds of Thy word, the servitors of Thy work.

With a calm and pure devotion we hail Thee and recognise Thee as the sole reality of our being.

February 11, 1914

As soon as one rises above the perception of contingencies, as soon as one's consciousness is identified with Thy supreme consciousness and one enters thus into that omniscience which I cannot define except as absolute Knowledge, how easy and even a little childish seem all those problems about what should or should not be done, about all the resolutions to be taken.

From the standpoint of the eternal work, the one thing important is to become conscious of Thee, to identify oneself with Thee and to maintain that conscious identification constantly. But as to what best use can be made of our physical organism, Thy mode of manifestation upon earth, it is quite enough, when Thou alone art conscious within us, to turn the gaze to the body in order to know beyond all doubt what is the best thing it can do, what activity will most fully utilise all its energies.

And without attaching much importance to that activity, that altogether relative utilisation, one can take without any difficulty, any inner debate, decisions which, to the outer consciousness appear the boldest and most dangerous.

How simple everything is for him who sees all things from the height of Thy eternity!

I hail Thee, O Lord, with a joyful and trusting devotion. May the peace of Thy divine love be with all beings.

71

February 12, 1914

WHEN, conscious with Thy supreme consciousness, one considers all earthly circumstances, one sees their complete relativity and says, "To do this thing or that, after all that is not of much importance; yet a particular mode of action will be the best utilisation of a certain faculty, a certain temperament. All actions, whatever they may be, even the most contradictory in appearance, can be an expression of Thy law to the extent that they are infused with the consciousness of that law, which is not a law of practical application that can be translated into principles or rules in the ordinary human consciousness but a law of attitude, of a constant and prevailing consciousness, something that cannot be expressed in formulas but may be lived."

But as soon as one falls back into the ordinary consciousness, nothing should be treated lightly and with indifference, the least circumstances, the smallest acts have a great importance and should be seriously considered; for we must try at every moment to do that which will make the identification of our consciousness with the eternal consciousness easy, and avoid carefully all that could be an obstacle to this identification. It is then that the rules of conduct having as their foundation perfect personal disinterestedness should find their full value.

With peace in my heart, with light in my mind, the hope born of certitude in all my being, I greet Thee, O Lord, divine Master of eternal love.

Thou art the reason of our existence and our goal.

February 13, 1914

IN the silence of an intense concentration I would unite my consciousness with Thy absolute consciousness, I would identify myself with Thee, O sovereign Lord of our being, divine Master of love, so that Thy law may become clear and perceptible to us and we may live only by it and for it.

How beautiful, grand, simple and calm everything is in the hours when my thought takes its flight to Thee and unites with Thee! And from the day it becomes possible for us to keep this supreme clear-sightedness constantly, with what an airy and yet sure step we shall walk through life above all obstacles and unhesitatingly! For, — this I know through experience — all doubt, all hesitation ceases the very moment one is conscious of Thy law; and if one perceives clearly the extreme relativity of all human action, one knows at the same time, with exactitude and precision, which action is the least relative in regard to one's body and one's own way of acting . . . and all obstacles *really* vanish as if by magic. All our efforts, O Lord, will henceforth be bent on an ever more constant realisation of this marvellous state.

May the peace of Thy certitude awaken in every heart!

February 14, 1914*

PEACE, peace upon all the earth!

May all escape from the ordinary consciousness and be delivered from the attachment for material things; may they awake to the knowledge of Thy divine presence, unite themselves with Thy supreme consciousness and taste the plenitude of peace that springs from it.

Lord, Thou art the sovereign Master of our being. Thy law is our law, and with all our strength we aspire to identify our consciousness with Thy eternal consciousness, that we may accomplish Thy sublime work in each thing and at every moment.

Lord, deliver us from all care for contingencies, deliver us from the ordinary outlook on things. Grant that we may henceforth see only with Thy eyes and act only by Thy will. Transform us into living torches of Thy divine love.

With reverence, with devotion, in a joyful consecration of my whole being I give myself, O Lord, to the fulfilment of Thy law.

Peace, peace upon all the earth!

February 15, 1914*

O THOU, sole Reality, Light of our light and Life of our life, Love supreme, Saviour of the world, grant that more and more I may be perfectly awakened to the awareness of Thy constant presence. Let all my acts conform to Thy law; let there be no difference between my will and Thine. Extricate me from the illusory consciousness of my mind, from its world of fantasies; let me identify my consciousness with the Absolute Consciousness, for that art Thou.

Give me constancy in the will to attain the end, give me firmness and energy and the courage which shakes off all torpor and lassitude.

Give me the peace of perfect disinterestedness, the peace that makes Thy presence felt and Thy intervention effective, the peace that is ever victorious over all bad will and every obscurity.

Grant, I implore Thee, that all in my being may be identified with Thee. May I be nothing else any more than a flame of love utterly awakened to a supreme realisation of Thee.

February 16, 1914

O SUPREME, sole Reality, true Consciousness, permanent Oneness, sovereign repose of perfect light, with what an intensity I aspire to be conscious of only Thee, to be only Thyself. This incessant whirl of unreal personalities, this multiplicity, this complexity, this excessive inextricable confusion of conflicting thoughts, struggling tendencies, battling desires, seems to me more and more frightful. I must emerge from this raging sea, land on Thy serene and peaceful shore. Give me the energy of an indefatigable swimmer. I would conquer Thee however great may be the effort needed for that. . . . O Lord, ignorance must be vanquished, illusion dispelled, this sorrowful universe must come out of its hideous nightmare, end its terrible dream, and awaken at last to the consciousness of Thy sole Reality.

O immutable Peace, deliver men from ignorance; may Thy plenary and pure Light reign everywhere!

February 17, 1914

O LORD, how ardently my aspiration rises to Thee: give us the full consciousness of Thy law, the constant perception of Thy will, so that our decision may be Thy decision and our life solely consecrated to Thy service and as perfect an expression as possible of Thy inspiration.

O Lord, dispel all darkness, all blindness; may every one enjoy the calm certitude that Thy divine illumination brings!

February 19, 1914

O LORD, be ever present in my thought! Not that I ask this of Thee, for I know that Thy Presence is constant and sovereign, I know that all we see and all that escapes our sight is just what it is only through Thy marvellous intervention, because of Thy divine law of love; but I say this and repeat it, I implore, in order to escape from forgetfulness and negligence.

Oh! to become Thy living love so powerfully as to transfigure and illumine all things, so completely as to awaken peace and benevolent satisfaction in all.

Oh, to become Thy divine love, pure and clearsighted, to be that always and everywhere! . . .

February 20, 1914

THE only thing that is important, the one thing that counts, is the will to be identified more and more completely with Thee, to unite our consciousness with Thy absolute Consciousness, to be more and more the peaceful, calm, disinterested, strong servitor of Thy sovereign law, Thy loving Will.

O Lord, give me the peace of perfect disinterestedness, the peace which makes Thy Presence effective, Thy intervention efficacious, the Peace ever triumphant over all bad will, all obscurity.

Lord, very humbly I pray to Thee that I may be equal to my task, that nothing in me, conscious or unconscious, may betray Thee by neglecting to serve Thy sacred mission.

In a silent devotion, I bow to Thee. . . .

February 21, 1914

EVERY day, every moment should be an occasion for a new and completer consecration, and not one of those enthusiastic and flurried consecrations, over-active, full of illusions about the work, but a deep and silent consecration which is not necessarily visible but penetrates and transfigures all action. Our mind, solitary and peaceful, should always repose in Thee and from that pure summit have the exact perception of realities, of the sole and eternal Reality behind all unstable and fleeting appearances.

O Lord, my heart is purified of all uneasiness and anguish; it is steady and calm and sees Thee in all things; and whatever our outer actions may be, whatever the circumstances the future has in store for us, I know that Thou alone livest, that Thou alone art real in Thy immutable permanence and it is in Thee that we live. . . .

May there be peace upon all the earth.

February 22, 1914

Wᴴᴱɴ I was a child of about thirteen, for nearly a year every night as soon as I had gone to bed it seemed to me that I went out of my body and rose straight up above the house, then above the city, very high above. Then I used to see myself clad in a magnificent golden robe, much longer than myself; and as I rose higher, the robe would stretch, spreading out in a circle around me to form a kind of immense roof over the city. Then I would see men, women, children, old men, the sick, the unfortunate coming out from every side; they would gather under the outspread robe, begging for help, telling of their miseries, their suffering, their hardships. In reply, the robe, supple and alive, would extend towards each one of them individually, and as soon as they had touched it, they were comforted or healed, and went back into their bodies happier and stronger than they had come out of them. Nothing seemed more beautiful to me, nothing could make me happier; and all the activities of the day seemed dull and colourless and without any real life, beside this activity of the night which was the true life for me. Often while I was rising up in this way, I used to see at my left an old man, silent and still, who looked at me with kindly affection and encouraged me by his presence. This old man, dressed in a long dark purple robe, was the personification — as I came to know later — of him who is called the Man of Sorrows.

Now that deep experience, that almost inexpressible reality, is translated in my mind by other ideas which I may describe in this way:

Many a time in the day and night it seems to me that I am, or rather my consciousness is, concentrated entirely in my heart which is no longer an organ, not even a feeling, but the divine Love, impersonal, eternal; and being this Love I feel myself living at the centre of each thing upon the entire earth, and at the same time I seem to stretch out immense, infinite arms and envelop with a boundless tenderness all beings, clasped, gathered, nestled on my breast that is vaster than the universe. . . . Words are poor and clumsy, O divine Master, and mental transcriptions are always childish. . . . But my aspiration to Thee is constant, and truly speaking, it is very often Thou and Thou alone who livest in this body, this imperfect means of manifesting Thee.

May all beings be happy in the peace of Thy illumination!

February 23, 1914

GRANT O Lord, that we may be more and more conscious of Thy law, that is, be one with it, so that we may foster its manifestation in all things.

Lord, grant that I may become master of my vagabond thought, that living in Thee I may see life only through Thee, and the illusion of material reality may come to an end and be replaced by a perception more in conformity with Thy eternal reality.

Let me live constantly in Thy divine Love, so that it may live in me and through me.

Grant that I may be an efficient and clear-sighted collaborator and that everything within me may foster the plenitude of Thy manifestation.

I know all my imperfections, my difficulties, my weaknesses, I feel all my ignorance, but I put my full trust in Thee and bow down before Thee in silent devotion.

February 25-26, 1914

HE who wants to serve Thee worthily should not be attached to anything, not even to those activities which enable him to commune more consciously with Thee. . . . But if as a result of the totality of circumstances, material things still take a greater place in life than usual, one must know how not to become absorbed by them, how to keep in one's inmost heart the clear vision of Thy presence and live constantly in that serene peace which nothing can disturb. . . .

Oh, to do everything seeing only Thee everywhere and thus soar above the act that has been carried out, without letting any chain that holds us prisoners to the earth burden our flight. . . .

O Lord, grant that the offering I make to Thee of my being may be integral and effective.

With a respectful and loving devotion I bow down before Thee, O ineffable Essence, inconceivable Reality, Nameless One.

February 27, 1914

O LORD, I sense the infinite happiness which is the portion of those whose life is entirely consecrated to Thee. And this does not depend upon outer circumstances but on one's own state of being and its greater or lesser degree of illumination. A perfect consecration to Thy law cannot but bring about modifications in the totality of circumstances, yet it is not these which make possible and express this perfect consecration. I mean that it is not under certain circumstances, always the same for all, that Thy law is manifested; for every one this manifestation is different according to his temperament, that is, according to the mission which for the moment is assigned to him in physical life.

But what is unchangeable and universal is the happy peace, the luminous and immutable serenity of all those who are solely consecrated to Thee, who no longer have any darkness, ignorance, egoistic attachment or bad will in them.

Oh, may all awake to this divine peace.

March 1, 1914

IT is in one's own self that all the obstacles lie, it is in one's own self that all the difficulties are found, it is in one's own self that there is all the darkness and ignorance. Were we to travel throughout the earth, were we to go and bury ourselves in some solitude, break with all our habits, lead the most ascetic life, yet if some bond of illusion held back our consciousness far from Thy absolute Consciousness, if some egoistic attachment cut us off from the integral communion with Thy divine Love, we would be no nearer Thee despite all outer circumstances. Can any circumstances be considered more or less favourable? I doubt it; it is the idea we have about them which enables us to profit much or little by the lessons they give us.

O Lord, I implore Thee! Grant that I may be perfectly conscious and master of all that constitutes this personality, so that I may be delivered from myself and Thou alone mayst live and act through these multiple elements.

To live in Love, by Love, for Love, indissolubly united to Thy highest manifestation. . . .

Always more light, more beauty, more truth!

March 3, 1914

As the day of departure draws near, I enter into a kind of self-communion; I turn with a fond solemnity towards all those thousand little nothings around us which have silently, for so many years, played their role of faithful friends; I thank them gratefully for all the charm they were able to give to the outer side of our life; I wish that if they are destined to pass into other hands than ours for any length of time, these hands may be gentle to them and know all the respect that is due to what Thy divine Love, O Lord, has brought out from the dark inconscience of chaos.

Then I turn towards the future and my gaze becomes more solemn still. What it holds in store for us I do not know nor care to know; outer circumstances have no importance at all; my only wish is that this may be for us the beginning of a new inner period in which, more detached from material things, we could be more conscious of Thy law and more one-pointedly consecrated to its manifestation; that it may be a period of greater light, greater love, of a more perfect dedication to Thy cause.

In a silent adoration I contemplate Thee. . . .

March 4, 1914

IT is likely to be the last time for a long while that I am writing at this table, in this calm room all charged with Thy Presence. For the next three days I shall probably not be able to write. . . . In an indrawn state I contemplate this turning page, vanishing into the dream of the past and look at the new page all full potentially of the dream of the future. . . . And yet how trifling this seems, how childish and unimportant, when seen in the light of Thy eternity. The only thing that is important is to obey Thy law with love and joy.

O Lord, grant that everything in us may adore and serve Thee.

May Peace be with all!

Geneva, March 6, 1914

AFTER having suffered acutely from their suffering, I turned towards Thee, trying to heal it by infusing into it a little of that divine Love which is the source of all peace and all happiness. We must not run away from suffering, we must not love and cultivate it either, we must learn how to go deep down into it sufficiently to turn it into a lever powerful enough for us to force open the doors of the eternal consciousness and enter the serenity of Thy unchanging Oneness.

Surely this sentimental and physical attachment which causes an agonizing wrench when bodies are separated, is childish from a certain point of view, when we contemplate the impermanence of outer forms and the reality of Thy essential Oneness; but, on the other hand, is not this attachment, this personal affection, an unconscious effort in men to realise outwardly, as far as possible, that fundamental oneness towards which they always move without even being aware of it? And precisely because of that, is not the suffering that separation brings one of the most effective means of transcending this outer consciousness, of replacing this superficial attachment by the integral realisation of Thy eternal Oneness?

This is what I wished for them all; this is what I ardently willed for them, and that is why, assured of Thy victory, certain of Thy triumph, I confided their grief to Thee that by illuminating it Thou mayst heal it.

O Lord, grant that all this beauty of affection and tenderness may be transformed into glorious knowledge. Grant that the best may emerge from everything and Thy happy Peace reign over the earth.

90

On board the "Kaga Maru", March 7, 1914

THOU wert with us yesterday as the most marvellous of protections; Thou didst permit Thy law to triumph even in the most external manifestation. Violence was answered by calm, brutality by the strength of sweetness; and where an irreparable disaster would have occurred, Thy power was glorified. O Lord, with what fervent gratitude did I greet Thy Presence. It was for me the sure sign that we would have the strength to act, to think, to live in Thy name and for Thee; not only in intention and will, but effectively in an integral realisation.

This morning my prayer rises to Thee, always with the same aspiration: to live Thy love, to radiate Thy love, with such potency and effectiveness that all may feel fortified, regenerated and illumined by our contact. To have power to heal life, to relieve suffering, to generate peace and calm confidence, to efface anguish and replace it by the sense of the one true happiness, the happiness that is founded in Thee and never fades. . . . O Lord, O marvellous Friend, O all-powerful Master, penetrate all our being, transfigure it till Thou alone livest in us and through us!

March 8, 1914*

IN front of this calm sunrise which turned all within me into silence and peace, at the moment when I grew conscious of Thee and Thou alone wast living in me, O Lord, it seemed to me that I adopted all the inhabitants of this ship, and enveloped them in an equal love, and that so in each one of them something of Thy consciousness would awake. Not often had I felt so strongly Thy divine power and Thy invincible light, and once again total was my confidence and unmixed my joyful surrender.

O Thou who relievest all suffering and dispersest all ignorance, O Thou the supreme healer, be constantly present on this boat in the heart of those whom it shelters that once again Thy glory may be manifested!

March 9, 1914*

THOSE who live for Thee and in Thee may change their physical surroundings, their habits, climate, "milieu", but everywhere they find the same atmosphere; they carry that atmosphere in themselves, in their thought constantly fixed on Thee. Everywhere they feel at home, for everywhere they are in Thy house. No longer do they marvel at the novelty, unexpectedness, picturesqueness of things and countries; for them, it is Thy Presence that is manifest in all and Thy unchangeable splendour, which never leaves them, is apparent in the least grain of sand. The whole earth chants Thy praises; in spite of the obscurity, misery, ignorance, through it all, it is still the glory of Thy love which we perceive and with which we can commune ceaselessly everywhere.

O Lord, my sweet Master, all this I constantly experience on this boat which seems to me a marvellous abode of peace, a temple sailing in Thy honour over the waves of the subconscient passivity which we have to conquer and awaken to the consciousness of Thy divine Presence.

Blessed was the day when I came to know Thee, O Ineffable Eternity.

Blessed among all days be that day when the earth at last awakened shall know Thee and shall live only for Thee.

March 10, 1914

IN the silence of the night Thy Peace reigned over all things, in the silence of my heart Thy Peace reigns always; and when these two silences were united, Thy Peace was so powerful that no disturbance of any kind could resist it. Then I thought of all those who were watching over the boat to safeguard and protect our course, and in gratefulness I wanted to make Thy Peace spring up and live in their hearts; then I thought of all those who, confident and free from care, slept the sleep of inconscience, and with solicitude for their miseries, pity for their latent suffering which would arise in them when they awoke, I wanted that a little of Thy Peace might live in their hearts and awaken in them the life of the spirit, the light that dispels ignorance. Then I thought of all the inhabitants of this vast sea, both visible and invisible, and I willed that Thy Peace might spread over them. Then I thought of those we had left far behind and whose affection goes with us, and with a great tenderness I wanted Thy conscious and lasting Peace for them, the plenitude of Thy Peace as far as they could receive it. Then I thought of all those towards whom we are going, who are troubled by childish preoccupations and fight in ignorance and egoism for petty rivalries of interest; and ardently, in a great aspiration, I asked for them the full light of Thy Peace. Then I thought of all those we know, all those we do not know, all the life in the making, all that has changed its form, all that is not yet in form, and for all these, even as for all that I cannot think about, for all that is present to my memory and for all that I forget, in a deep contemplation and mute adoration I implored Thy Peace.

March 12, 1914

O LORD, my one aspiration is to know Thee and serve Thee better every day. What do outer circumstances matter? They seem to me each day more vain and illusory, and I take less and less interest in what is going to happen to us in the outer life; but more and more am I intensely interested in the one thing which seems important to me: to know Thee better in order to serve Thee better. All outer events must converge upon this goal and this goal alone; and for that all depends upon the attitude we have towards them. To seek Thee constantly in all things, to want to manifest Thee ever better in every circumstance, in this attitude lies supreme Peace, perfect serenity, true contentment. In it life blossoms, widens, expands so magnificently in such majestic waves that no storm can any longer disturb it.

O Lord, Thou art our safeguard, our only happiness, Thou art our resplendent light, our pure love, our hope and our strength. Thou art our life, the reality of our being!

In a reverent and joyful adoration I bow to Thee.

March 13, 1914

HOW many different levels there are in consciousness! This word should be reserved for what is illumined in a being by Thy Presence, is identified with Thee and partakes of Thy absolute Consciousness, for that which has knowledge, that which is "perfectly awakened", as the Buddha says.

Outside this state there are infinite grades of consciousness, going right down to complete darkness, the veritable inconscience which may be a domain yet untouched by the light of Thy divine Love (but this seems improbable in physical substance), or which is, for some kind of reason of ignorance, outside our individual range of perception.

This is, however, only a way of speaking, and a very incomplete one; for when the being becomes aware of Thy presence and is identified with Thy consciousness, it is conscious in all things and everywhere. But the fleeting duration of this supreme consciousness can be explained only by the complexity of the elements of the being, by their unequal illumination and by the fact that they enter into activity successively. It is, moreover, because of this successive activity that they can gradually become aware of themselves as a result of their experiences, both objective and subjective (which are really one and the same), that is, discover Thee in their unfathomable essence.

The subconscient is the intermediate zone between precise perception and ignorance, total darkness; it is probable that most beings, even human beings, live constantly in this subconscient; few emerge from it. This is the conquest that is to be made; for to be conscious in the true sense of the word is to be Thyself integrally; and is not this the very definition of the work to be accomplished, the mission to be fulfilled upon earth?

Deliver us, O Lord, from darkness; grant that we may become perfectly awake....

Sweet Master of Love, grant that all my consciousness may be concentrated in Thee so that I may live only by love and light and that love and light may radiate through me and awaken in all on our journey; may this physical journey be like a symbol of our action and may we leave everywhere a trace of Thee like a trail of light and love.

O divine Master, eternal Teacher, Thou livest in all things, in all beings, and Thy love bursts upon the sight of even the most ignorant. Grant that all may become aware of it in the depths of their being and that hatred may disappear for ever from their hearts.

My ardent gratitude rises to Thee like a tireless chant.

March 14, 1914

IN the immutable solitude of the desert there is something of Thy majestic presence, and I understand why one of the best means of finding Thee has always been to withdraw into these immense stretches of sand.

But for one who knows Thee, Thou art everywhere, in all things, and none of them seems more suitable than another for manifesting Thee; for all things that exist — and many others that yet do not — are necessary to express Thee. Each thing, by virtue of Thy divine intervention of love, is an effort of life towards Thee; and as soon as our eyes are unsealed, we perceive this effort constantly.

O Lord, my heart is athirst for Thee and my thought seeks for Thee constantly. In a mute adoration I bow to Thee.

March 15, 1914

MY thought is filled with Thee, my heart is full, all my being is filled with Thy Presence, and peace grows ever deeper, giving rise to that happiness, so special, so unmixed, of a calm serenity, which seems vast as the universe, deep as the unfathomable depths which lead to Thee.

Oh, these silent and pure nights when my heart overflows and unites with Thy divine Love to penetrate all things, embrace all life, illumine and regenerate all thought, purify all feeling, awaken in every being the consciousness of Thy marvellous Presence and of the ineffable peace that flows from it!

Grant, O Lord, that this consciousness and peace may constantly grow within us, so that we may be more and more the faithful intermediaries of Thy divine and absolute law.

March 17, 1914

WHEN physical conditions are a little difficult and some discomfort follows, if one knows how to surrender completely before Thy will, caring little for life or death, health or illness, the integral being enters immediately into harmony with Thy law of love and life, and all physical indisposition ceases giving place to a calm well-being, deep and peaceful.

I have noticed that when one enters into an activity that necessitates great physical endurance, what tires one most is anticipating beforehand all the difficulties to which one will be exposed. It is much wiser to see at every moment only the difficulty of the present instant; in this way the effort becomes much easier for it is always proportionate to the amount of strength, the resistance at one's disposal. The body is a marvellous tool, it is our mind that does not know how to use it and, instead of fostering its suppleness, its plasticity, it brings a certain fixity into it which comes from preconceived ideas and unfavourable suggestions.

But the supreme science, O Lord, is to unite with Thee, to trust in Thee, to live in Thee, to be Thyself; and then nothing is any longer impossible to a man who manifests Thy omnipotence.

Lord, my aspiration rises to Thee like a silent canticle, a mute adoration, and Thy divine Love illumines my heart.

O divine Master, I bow to Thee!

March 18, 1914

THOU art perfect knowledge, absolute consciousness. He who unites with Thee is omniscient — while the union lasts. But even before attaining this stage, he who has given himself to Thee in all the sincerity of his being, with all his conscious will, he who has resolved to make every effort to help in the manifestation and triumph of Thy divine law of Love in himself and the whole field of his influence, sees all things in his life change, and all circumstances begin to express Thy law and assist his consecration; for him it is the best, the very best that always happens; and if in his intelligence there is still some obscurity, some ignorant desire which at times prevents him from becoming aware of it immediately, he recognises sooner or later that a beneficent power seemed to protect him even from himself and secure for him conditions most favourable to his blossoming and transfiguration, his integral conversion and utilisation.

As soon as one becomes conscious and convinced of this, one can no longer worry about future circumstances or the turn events take; it is with perfect serenity that one does at every moment what one thinks best, convinced that the best too is sure to come from it, even if it is not the result which we, with our limited reasoning, expected from it.

That is why, Lord, our heart is light, our thought in repose. That is why we turn to Thee in all confidence and say peacefully:

May Thy will be done, in it true harmony is realised.

March 19, 1914

O LORD, eternal Teacher, Thou whom we can neither name nor understand, but whom we want to realise more and more at every moment, enlighten our intelligence, illumine our hearts, transfigure our consciousness; may everyone awaken to the true life, flee from egoism and its train of sorrow and anguish, and take refuge in Thy divine and pure Love, source of all peace and all happiness. My heart so full of Thee seems to expand into infinity and my intelligence, all illumined with Thy Presence, shines like the purest diamond. Thou art the wonderful magician, he who transfigures all things, from ugliness brings forth beauty, from darkness light, from the mud clear water, from ignorance knowledge and from egoism goodness.

In Thee, by Thee, for Thee we live and Thy law is the supreme master of our life.

May Thy will be done in every place, may Thy peace reign upon all the earth.

March 20, 1914

THOU art consciousness and light, Thou art peace in the depth of all things, the divine love that transfigures, the knowledge that triumphs over darkness. To feel Thee and aspire to Thee one should have emerged from the immense sea of the subconscient, one should have begun to crystallise, to grow distinct so as to know oneself and then give oneself as that alone which is its own master can do. And what effort and struggle it takes to attain this crystallisation, to emerge from the amorphous state of the environment; and how much more effort and struggle yet to give oneself, to surrender once the individuality has been formed.

Few beings consent willingly to make this effort; so life with its brutal unforeseen events obliges men to make it unintentionally, for they cannot do otherwise. And little by little Thy work is accomplished despite all obstacles.

March 21, 1914

EVERY morning my aspiration rises ardently to Thee, and in the silence of my satisfied heart I ask that Thy law of Love may be expressed, that Thy will may manifest. And in anticipation I adhere with joy and serenity to those circumstances which will express this law and this will.

Oh, why be restless and want that for oneself things should turn out in one way and not another! Why decide that a particular set of circumstances will be the expression of the best possibilities and then launch into a bitter struggle so that these possibilities may be realised! Why not use all one's energy solely to will in the calm of inner confidence that Thy law may triumph everywhere and always over all difficulties, all darkness, all egoism! How the horizon widens as soon as one learns to take this attitude; how all anxiety vanishes giving place to a constant illumination, to the omnipotence of disinterestedness! To will what Thou willest, O Lord, is to live constantly in communion with Thee, to be delivered from all contingencies, to escape all narrowness, to fill one's lungs with pure and wholesome air, to get rid of all useless weariness, be relieved of all cumbrous loads, so as to run briskly towards the only goal worth attaining: the triumph of Thy divine Law!

O Lord, with what joy and trust I greet Thee this morning! . . .

March 22, 1914

O LORD, divine Master of Love, enlighten their consciousness and their hearts. They have made an effort to reach out towards Thee but because of their ignorance their prayers probably did not rise to Thee, and their false conceptions have barred the way to their aspiration. Yet in Thy mercy Thou dost turn all goodwill to account and a flash of sincerity is enough for Thy divine light to use it to illumine the intelligence, for Thy sublime love to penetrate into all hearts and fill them with that pure and lofty benevolence which is one of the best expressions of Thy law. What I willed for them, with Thy will, in moments when I could be in true communion with Thee — grant that they may have received it on the day when, striving to forget all outer contingencies, they turned to their noblest thought, their best feelings.

May the supreme serenity of Thy sublime Presence awake in them.

March 23, 1914

As I see it, the ideal state is that in which, constantly conscious with Thy Consciousness, one knows at every moment, spontaneously, without any reflection being necessary, exactly what should be done to best express Thy law. That state I know, for I have experienced it at certain moments, but very often the knowledge of the "how" is veiled by a mist of ignorance and one must call in reflection which is not always a good counsellor — let alone all that one does at every instant without having any time for reflection, on the spur of the moment. How far does it conform with or oppose Thy law? That depends upon the state of the subconscient, on what is active in it at that time. Once the deed is done, if it has any importance, if one can look at it, analyse it, understand it, it serves as a lesson, enables one to become aware of one's motive of action and hence of something in the subconscient which still governs the being and has to be mastered.

Every action on earth is bound to have a good and a bad side. Even the actions which best express the most divine law of Love carry in them something of the disorder and darkness inherent in the world as it is today. Some people, those who are called pessimists, perceive almost exclusively the dark side of everything. The optimists, on the other hand, see only the side of beauty and harmony. And if it is foolish and ignorant to be an unwitting optimist, is it not making a happy conquest to become a willing optimist? In the eyes of pessimists, whatever one does will always be bad, ignorant or egoistic; how could one satisfy them? It is an impossible task.

There is only one recourse; to unite as perfectly as possible with the highest and purest light that one can conceive, to identify one's consciousness as completely as possible with the absolute Consciousness, to strive to receive all inspirations from that Consciousness alone so as to foster as best one can its manifestation upon earth, and, trusting in its power, to regard all events with serenity.

Since everything is necessarily mixed in the present manifestation, the wisest thing is to do one's best, striving towards an ever higher light and to resign oneself to the fact that absolute perfection is for the moment unrealisable.

And yet how ardently must we always aspire for that inaccessible perfection! . . .

March 24, 1914

THE result of all my reflections of yesterday is the finding that the only disturbance I experience comes from my
fear of not having been or of not being perfectly identified
with Thy law. And this disturbance comes precisely from
the fact that the identification is not complete; for if it
were, I could not ask myself whether it is so and, on the
other hand, as I know from experience, all disturbance
would become impossible for me.

But in face of an error or blunder, the true thought to
have is not to say to oneself, "I should have done better, I
should have done this instead of that", but rather "I was
not sufficiently identified with the eternal Consciousness,
I must strive to realise better this definitive and integral
union."

Yesterday afternoon, during those long hours of silent
contemplation, I understood at last what is meant by true
identification with the object of one's thought. I touched
this realisation, as it were, not by achieving a mental state,
but simply through steadiness and control of thought. I
understood that I would need long, very long hours of
contemplation to be able to perfect this realisation. This
is one of the things I expect from the journey to India, if
indeed Thou dost consider it useful for Thy service, Lord.

My progress is slow, very slow, but I hope that in compensation it may be lasting and free from all fluctuation.

Grant that I may accomplish my mission, that I may
help in Thy integral manifestation.

March 25, 1914*

SILENT and unseen as always, but all-powerful, Thy action has made itself felt and, in these souls that seemed to be so closed, a perception of Thy divine light is awake. I knew well that none could invoke Thy presence in vain and if in the sincerity of our hearts we commune with Thee through no matter what organism, body or human collectivity, this organism in spite of its ignorance finds its unconsciousness wholly transformed. But when in one or several elements there is the conscious transformation, when the flame that smoulders under the ashes leaps out suddenly illumining all the being, then with joy we salute Thy sovereign action, testify once more to Thy invincible puissance and can hope that a new possibility of true happiness has been added to the others in mankind.

O Lord, an ardent thanksgiving mounts from me towards Thee expressing the gratitude of this sorrowing humanity which Thou illuminest, transformest and glorifiest and givest to it the peace of Knowledge.

March 28, 1914

FROM the time we started and every day more and more, in all things we can see Thy divine intervention, everywhere Thy law is expressed, and I need all my inner conviction to feel that this is perfectly natural, so that I do not pass from wonder to wonder.

At no moment do I feel that I am living outside Thee and never have the horizons appeared vaster to me and the depths at once more luminous and unfathomable. Grant, O Divine Teacher, that we may know and accomplish our mission upon earth better and better, more and more, that we may make full use of all the energies that are in us, and Thy sovereign Presence become manifest ever more perfectly in the silent depths of our soul, in all our thoughts, all our feelings, all our actions.

I find it almost strange to speak to Thee, so much is it Thou who livest in me, thinkest and lovest.

Pondicherry, March 29, 1914

O THOU whom we must know, understand, realise, absolute Consciousness, eternal Law, Thou who guidest and illuminest us, who movest and inspirest us, grant that these weak souls may be strengthened and those who fear be reassured. To Thee I entrust them, even as I entrust to Thee our entire destiny.

March 30, 1914

IN the presence of those who are integrally Thy servitors, those who have attained the perfect consciousness of Thy presence, I become aware that I am still far, very far from what I yearn to realise; and I know that the highest I can conceive, the noblest and purest is still dark and ignorant beside what I should conceive. But this perception, far from being depressing, stimulates and strengthens the aspiration, the energy, the will to triumph over all obstacles so as to be at last identified with Thy law and Thy work.

Gradually the horizon becomes distinct, the path grows clear, and we move towards a greater and greater certitude.

It matters little that there are thousands of beings plunged in the densest ignorance, He whom we saw yesterday is on earth; his presence is enough to prove that a day will come when darkness shall be transformed into light, and Thy reign shall be indeed established upon earth.

O Lord, Divine Builder of this marvel, my heart overflows with joy and gratitude when I think of it, and my hope has no bounds.

My adoration is beyond all words, my reverence is silent.

April 1, 1914

I FEEL we have entered the very heart of Thy sanctuary and grown aware of Thy very will. A great joy, a deep peace reign in me, and yet all my inner constructions have vanished like a vain dream and I find myself now, before Thy immensity, without a frame or system, like a being not yet individualised. All the past in its external form seems ridiculously arbitrary to me, and yet I know it was useful in its own time.

But now all is changed: a new stage has begun.

114

April 2, 1914

EVERY day, when I want to write, I am interrupted, as though the new period opening now before us were a period of expansion rather than of concentration. It is in the activity of each moment that we must serve Thee and identify ourselves with Thee rather than in deep and silent contemplation or in meditation, written or unwritten.

But my heart does not tire of singing a hymn to Thee and my thought is constantly filled with Thee.

April 3, 1914

IT seems to me that I am being born to a new life and all the methods, the habits of the past can no longer be of any use. It seems to me that what I thought were results is nothing more than a preparation. I feel as though I have done nothing yet, as though I have not lived the spiritual life, only entered the path that leads to it, it seems to me that I know nothing, that I am incapable of formulating anything, that all experience is yet to begin. It is as though I were stripped of my entire past, of its errors as well as its conquests, as though all that has vanished and made room for a new-born child whose whole existence is yet to be lived, who has no Karma, no experience to learn from, but no error either which has to be set right. My head is empty of all knowledge and all certitude, but also of all vain thought. I feel that if I learn how to surrender without any resistance to this state, if I do not try to know or understand, if I consent to be completely like an ignorant and candid child, some new possibility will open before me. I know that I must now definitively give myself up and be like an absolutely blank page on which Thy thought, Thy will, O Lord, can be inscribed freely without danger of any deformation.

An immense gratitude rises from my heart, it seems to me that I have at last reached the threshold I sought so much.

Grant, O Lord, that I may be sufficiently pure, impersonal, animated with Thy divine love to be able to cross it definitively.

Oh, to belong to Thee without any darkness, without any restriction!

April 4, 1914

O LORD, my adoration rises ardently to Thee, all my being is an aspiration, a flame consecrated to Thee.

Lord, Lord, my sweet Master, it is Thou who livest and willest in me!

This body is Thy instrument; this will is Thy servant; this intelligence is Thy tool; and the whole being is only Thyself.

April 7, 1914

W HAT kind of courage is mine that I always try to avoid the fight? What kind of energy is mine, that I am instinctively frightened of the new effort to be made and try, without being aware of it, to go to sleep passively, relying upon the results of previous efforts? In order to act, I have to be compelled and my mute contemplation is partly made of laziness. . . . All this is becoming more and more clearly apparent to me. All that I have done till now seems to me to be nothing. The poverty and limitations of the instrument I put at Thy service, Lord, are evident to me, and I laugh a little sorrowfully at the idea that at times I could have a good opinion of my being, its efforts and their results. This threshold of the true life that I always think I have reached is like a hope bestowed upon me but never a tangible realisation; it is the toy promised to a child, the reward held out for a moment before the weak.

When shall I become a truly strong being, made entirely of courage, energy, valour and calm perseverance; when shall I have forgotten my own person completely enough to be nothing but an instrument moulded solely by the forces it has to manifest? When will my consciousness of unity be no longer tinged with any inertia; when will my feeling of divine love be no longer mixed with any weakness?

O Lord, all thought seems dead within me, now that I have asked these questions. I search for my conscious mind and I do not find it; I search for my individuality and

119

I cannot discover it anywhere; I search for my personal will and it is not there. I search for Thee, and Thou art silent. . . . Silence, silence. . . .

Now I seem to hear Thy voice: "Never hast thou known how to die integrally. Always something in thee has wanted to know, to witness, to understand. Surrender completely, learn how to disappear, break the last barrier that separates thee from me; accomplish unreservedly thy act of surrender." Alas, O Lord, for a long time have I wanted it, but I could not. Now wilt Thou give me the power to do so?

O Lord, my sweet eternal Master, break this resistance which fills me with anguish . . . deliver me from myself!

April 8, 1914

LORD, my thought is calm and my heart ingathered; I turn towards Thee with a profound devotion and a boundless trust: I know that Thy love is all-powerful and that Thy justice will reign over the earth; I know that the hour is near when the last veil will be rent and all iniquity disappear to give place to an era of peace and harmonious effort.

O Lord, with thought rapt within and the heart at peace, I approach Thee and all my being is filled with Thy divine Presence; grant that I may see Thee alone in all things and that all may be resplendent with Thy divine Light. Oh, may all hatred be appeased, all rancour effaced, all fears dispelled, all suspicions destroyed, all malevolence overcome, and in this city, in this country, upon this earth, may all hearts feel vibrating within them that sublime love, source of all transfiguration.

O Lord, how ardently do I call and implore Thy love! Grant that my aspiration may be intense enough to awaken the same aspiration everywhere: oh, may goodness, justice and peace reign as supreme masters, may ignorant egoism be overcome, darkness be suddenly illuminated by Thy pure Light; may the blind see, the deaf hear, may Thy law be proclaimed in every place and, in a constantly progressive union, in an ever more perfect harmony, may all, like one single being, stretch out their arms towards Thee to identify themselves with Thee and manifest Thee upon earth.

O Lord, with thought rapt within, the heart radiant with sunshine, I give myself to Thee without reservation, and the "self" disappears in Thee!

April 10, 1914*

SUDDENLY the veil was rent, the horizon was disclosed — and before the clear vision my whole being threw itself at Thy feet in a great outburst of gratitude. Yet in spite of this deep and integral joy all was calm, all was peaceful with the peace of eternity.

I seem to have no more limits; there is no longer the perception of the body, no sensations, no feelings, no thoughts — a clear, pure, tranquil immensity penetrated with love and light, filled with an unspeakable beatitude is all that is there and that alone seems now to be myself, and this "myself" is so little the former "I", selfish and limited, that I cannot tell if it is I or Thou, O Lord, sublime Master of our destinies.

It is as though all were energy, courage, force, will, infinite sweetness, incomparable compassion. . . .

Even more forcibly than during these last days the past is dead and as though buried under the rays of a new life. The last glance that I have just thrown backward as I read a few pages of this book definitely convinced me of this death, and lightened of a great weight I present myself before Thee, O my divine Master, with all the simplicity, all the nudity of a child. . . . And still the one only thing I perceive is that calm and pure immensity. . . .

Lord, Thou hast answered my prayer, Thou hast granted me what I have asked from Thee; the "I" has disappeared, there is only a docile instrument put at Thy service, a centre of concentration and manifestation of Thy infinite and eternal rays; Thou hast taken my life and made it Thine; Thou hast taken my will and hast united it to Thine; Thou hast taken my love and identified it with Thine; Thou hast taken my thought and replaced it by Thy absolute consciousness.

The body, marvelling, bows its forehead in the dust in mute and submissive adoration.

And nothing else exists but Thou alone in the splendour of Thy immutable peace.

Karikal, April 13, 1914

EVERYTHING works together to prevent me from remaining a creature of habits, and in this new state, in the midst of these circumstances, so complex and unstable, I have never before so completely lived Thy immutable peace or rather the "I" has never before disappeared so completely that Thy divine peace alone is alive there. All is beautiful, harmonious and calm, all is full of Thee. Thou shinest in the dazzling sun, Thou art felt in the gentle passing breeze, Thou dost manifest Thyself in all hearts and live in all beings. There is not an animal, a plant that does not speak to me of Thee and Thy name is written upon everything I see.

O my sweet Lord, hast Thou at last granted that I may belong entirely to Thee and that my consciousness may be definitively united with Thine? What have I done to be worthy of so glorious a happiness? Nothing except to desire it, to want it with constancy — that is very little.

But, O Lord, since now it is Thy will and not mine that lives in me, Thou wilt be able to make this happiness profitable to all; and its very purpose will be to enable the greatest possible number of beings to perceive Thee.

Oh, may all know Thee, love Thee, serve Thee; may all receive the supreme consecration!

O Love, divine Love, spread abroad in the world, regenerate life, enlighten the intelligence, break the barriers of egoism, scatter the obstacles of ignorance, shine resplendent as sovereign Master of the earth.

125

Pondicherry, April 17, 1914 *

O LORD, O almighty Master, sole Reality, grant that no error, no obscurity, no fatal ignorance may creep into my heart and my thought.

In action, the personality is the inevitable and indispensable intermediary of Thy will and Thy forces.

The stronger, the more complex, powerful, individualised and conscious is the personality, the more powerfully and usefully can the instrument serve. But, by reason of the very character of personality, it easily tends to be drawn into the fatal illusion of its separate existence and become little by little a screen between Thee and that on which Thou willest to act. Not at the beginning, in the manifestation, but in the transmission of the return; that is to say, instead of being, as a faithful servant, an intermediary who brings back to Thee exactly what is Thy due — the forces sent forth in reply to Thy action, — there is a tendency in the personality to want to keep for itself a part of the forces, with this idea: "It is I who have done this or that, I who am thanked. . . . " Pernicious illusion, obscure falsehood, now are you discovered and unmasked. That is the maleficent canker corroding the fruit of the action, falsifying all its results.

O Lord, O my sweet Master, sole Reality, dispel this feeling of the "I". I have now understood that so long as there will be a manifested universe, the "I" will remain necessary for Thy manifestation; to dissolve, or even to diminish or weaken the "I", is to deprive Thee of the means of manifestation, in whole or part. But what must be radically and definitively suppressed is the illusory thought, the illusory feeling, the illusory sensation of the separate "I". At no moment, in no circumstances must we forget that our "I" has no reality outside Thee.

O my sweet Master, my divine Lord, tear out from my heart this illusion so that Thy servant may become pure and faithful and faithfully and integrally bring back to Thee all that is Thy due. In silence let me contemplate and understand this supreme ignorance and dispel it for ever. Chase the shadow from my heart, and let Thy light reign in it, its uncontested sovereign.

April 18, 1914

YESTERDAY morning the last veil was almost rent, the last stronghold of the blind and ignorant personality seemed to be on the point of yielding; for the first time I thought I had understood what true impersonal service was, and the obstacle separating me from the integral realisation seemed very fragile to me, and on the point of disappearing definitively. But the necessity of my outer duties tore me away from this beneficent and happy contemplation, and when I was obliged to return to the outer consciousness the veil closed again and now seems to me darker than ever. Why this fall into the inconscience of night after so great a light? . . .

O Lord, Lord, wilt Thou not then let me escape at last from ignorance and become one with Thee? Now that I have known and seen so well what the work upon the earth must be, could I not realise it? Am I then riveted to ignorance and illusion? . . .

Why, why this night after so great and pure a light? All my being is tense in a call of anguish!

O Lord, take pity on me!

April 19, 1914

THERE is a great difference between being in the midst of active work, of external action, while keeping one's thought constantly fixed on Thee, and entering into that perfect union with Thee which leads to what I have called "absolute Consciousness, true Omniscience, Knowledge". When one acts, though with the thought fixed on Thee, one is like a blind man walking on the road with a sense of direction, but knowing nothing about the path he is following and how, precisely, one must walk so as to neglect nothing. In the other case, on the contrary, there is the clear vision in full light, the utilisation of the least occasion, the plenitude of action, the maximum result. And if the first attitude is indispensable before acquiring the other, yet at no moment must one cease working, making an effort to attain perfect communion.

But my heart is in peace, my thought free from impatience, and I entrust myself to Thy will with the smiling confidence of a child.

May Thy peace reign over all. . . .

April 20, 1914

AFTER having hoped so much, after having believed that my outer being was at last to become an instrument adapted to Thy purpose, after feeling hopeful that I would at last be delivered from this obscure and cumbersome "self", I feel I am as far from the goal as before, as ignorant, as egoistic as I was before this great expectation. And the path stretches out once again, interminable across the fields of inconscience. The sublime door has closed again and I find myself still on the threshold of the sanctuary without being able to enter within. But I have learnt to look at everything with a smile and a tranquil heart. I ask only this of Thee, O my divine Master, not to let me make any mistakes; even if the instrument is still condemned for a time to unconsciousness, grant that it may let itself be guided faithfully and docilely by Thy divine law.

I bow to Thee, O Lord, with a deep and pure devotion. Oh! be the sovereign Master of all hearts.

April 23, 1914

ALL rules have vanished, the regularity of the discipline is gone, all effort has ceased; not by my own will nor, I believe, through negligence, but because circumstances are working together to bring this about. It seems that this inner will, always alert, like a steersman holding the rudder, has evaporated or fallen asleep, and my being is only something peacefully surrendered which lets itself be carried along by the stream. Till now, it seems to me, the course has always been in a straight line, and I would keep the hope that it is Thou, O Lord, who guidest the stream; but surely if I have erred at times through too great a rigidity, a lack of suppleness and spontaneity, it could very well be that now I err through the opposite excess. I have come to accept peacefully the state I am in and to tell myself that Thou wilt bestow upon me the true Consciousness, the absolute Consciousness when Thou thinkest it best.

I look at all this changing world as a game unfolding itself, and I take part in this game with the same energy and conviction with which I would if I believed it real and important. All this is very new. But what is certain is that never before were my mind and heart in so complete a repose. What will come out of that, I do not know. But I trust in Thee, O Lord; Thou knowest the best way of using and developing Thy instrument. . . .

April 28, 1914

THOU art the Master of the world; Thy law unfolds before us with precision, and as I thought or rather as Thou didst make me understand it before we left Paris, it is the best — what could best serve Thy work in the world — that has happened.

In beatitude I communed with Thy puissance dominating over darkness and error, shining like a marvellous and eternal dawn above the mud of hypocritical force and its apparent success. Everything has been brought to light, we have taken one more step towards the full light of sincerity, and this full light will be the first stage of Thy reign upon earth.

O Thou inconceivable splendour, Thou conqueror of all ignorance, victor over all egoism, Thou who dost illumine all hearts and enlighten all minds, Thou who art Knowledge and Love and Being, let me live constantly in the consciousness of Thy unity, let me always conform to Thy Will.

With reverent and silent devotion I bow to Thee as the sovereign Lord of the world.

May 2, 1914

BEYOND all human conceptions, even the most marvellous, beyond all human feelings, even the most sublime, beyond the most magnificent aspirations and the purest flights, beyond Love, Knowledge and the Oneness of Being, I would enter into constant communion with Thee, O Lord. Free from all shackles I shall be Thyself; it will be Thou who wilt see the world through this body; it will be Thou who wilt act in the world through this instrument.

In me is the calm serenity of perfect certitude.

May 3, 1914

O DIVINE Love, supreme Knowledge, perfect One-ness, at every moment of the day I call to Thee so as to be nothing but Thou alone!

May this instrument serve Thee, conscious of being an instrument, and may all my consciousness, merged in Thine, contemplate all things with Thy divine vision.

O Lord, Lord, grant that Thy sovereign Power may manifest; grant that Thy work may be accomplished and Thy servitor be consecrated solely to Thy service.

May the "I" disappear for evermore, may only the instrument remain.

May 4, 1914

To be merged both in Thee and in Thy work . . . to be no longer a limited individuality . . . to become the infinitude of Thy forces manifesting through one point . . . to be freed from all shackles and all limitations . . . to rise above all restrictive thought . . . to act while remaining outside the action . . . to act with and for individuals while seeing only Oneness, the Oneness of Thy Love, Thy Knowledge, Thy Being . . . O my divine Master, eternal Teacher, Sole Reality, dispel all darkness in this aggregate Thou hast formed for Thy service, Thy manifestation in the world. Realise in it that supreme consciousness which will awaken the same consciousness everywhere.

Oh, no longer to see appearances which incessantly change; always to contemplate in everything and everywhere only Thy immutable Oneness!

O Lord, all my being cries to Thee in an irresistible call; wilt Thou not grant that I may become Thyself in my integral consciousness, since in truth I am Thou and Thou art I?

May 9, 1914

JUST at the moment when I was feeling the imperious need of resuming these notes regularly so as to come out of this overwhelming mental inertia, my physical organism suffered a defeat such as it had not known for several years and during a few days all the forces of my body failed me; I saw in this a sign that I had made a mistake, that my spiritual energy had weakened, my vision of the omnipotent Oneness had been clouded, that some wrong suggestion had managed to disturb me in some way, and I bowed down before Thee, O Lord, my sweet Master, with humility, conscious that I was not yet ready for a perfect identification with Thee. Something in this aggregate which constitutes the instrument I can put at Thy service is still obscure and obtuse; something does not respond as it should to Thy forces, deforms and darkens their manifestation. . . .

A great problem came up before me and illness covered it with its veil and prevented me from solving it. Now that I am living once more in the feeling of Thy Oneness, the problem no longer seems to have any sense and I do not understand it very well any more.

It seems to me I have left something far behind me, it seems to me that I am slowly awakening to a new life. I would it were not an illusion and this deep and smiling peace had returned forever.

O my divine Master, my love aspires to Thee more intensely than ever; let me be Thy living Love in the world and nothing but that! May all egoism, all limitation, all darkness disappear; may my consciousness be identified with Thine so that Thou alone mayst be the will acting through this fragile and transient instrument.

O my sweet Master, how ardently my love aspires to Thee. . . .

Grant that I may be nothing but Thy Divine Love and that in every being this Love may awake, powerful and victorious.

Let me be a vast mantle of love enveloping all the earth, entering all hearts, murmuring in every ear Thy divine message of hope and peace.

O my divine Master, how ardently I aspire for Thee! Break these chains of darkness and error; dispel this ignorance, liberate, liberate me, make me see Thy light. . . .

Break, break these chains. . . . I want to understand and I want to be. That is to say, this "I" must be Thy "I" and there must be only one single "I" in the world.

O Lord, grant my prayer, my supplication rises ardently to Thee.

May 10, 1914

IT is Thy sweet joy, O Lord, that fills my heart; it is Thy silent peace that reigns over my mind. All is repose, force, concentration, light and serenity; and all this is without any limit, without any division; is it only the earth or rather the whole universe that lives in me, I do not know; but it is Thou, O Lord, who dwellest in this consciousness and givest it life; it is Thou who seest, knowest, actest. It is Thou alone whom I see everywhere, or rather there is no longer any "I", all is one and this Oneness is Thou.

Glory to Thee, O Lord, Master of the world, Thou shinest resplendent in all things!

May 12, 1914*

MORE and more it seems to me that we are in one of those periods of activity in which the fruit of past efforts becomes apparent, — a period in which we act according to Thy law in the measure in which it is the sovereign controller of our being, without having even the leisure to become conscious of the law.

This morning passing by a rapid experience from depth to depth, I was able, once again, as always, to identify my consciousness with Thine and to live no longer in aught but Thee; — indeed, it was Thou alone that wast living, but immediately Thy will pulled my consciousness towards the exterior, towards the work to be done, and Thou saidst to me, "Be the instrument of which I have need." And is not this the last renunciation, to renounce identification with Thee, to renounce the sweet and pure joy of no longer distinguishing between Thee and me, the joy of knowing at each moment, not only with the intellect but by an integral experience, that Thou art the unique Reality and that all the rest is but appearance and illusion. That the exterior being should be the docile instrument which does not even need to be conscious of the will which moves it, is not doubtful; but why must I be almost entirely identified with the instrument and why should not the "I" be entirely merged in Thee and live Thy full and absolute consciousness?

I ask, but I am not anxious about it. I know that all is according to Thy will, and with a pure adoration I trust myself joyously to Thy will. I shall be what Thou wouldst have me be, O Lord, conscient or inconscient, a simple instrument as is the body or a supreme knowledge as art Thou. O the sweet and peaceful joy when one can say "All is good" and feel Thee at work in the world through all the elements which lend themselves to that transmission.

Thou art the sovereign Master of all, Thou art the Inaccessible, the Unknowable, the eternal and sublime Reality.

O marvellous Unity, I disappear in Thee.

May 13, 1914

THIS somnolence of my thought, O Lord, Thou wilt shake off so that I may have the knowledge and understand the experience Thou hast given to my being. When something in me questions Thee, always Thou repliest, and when it is necessary for me to know something, Thou teachest it to me, whether directly or indirectly.

I see more and more that all impatient revolt, all haste would be useless; everything is slowly organised so that I may serve Thee as I should. What is my place in this service? For a long time I have stopped asking myself this. What does it matter? Is it necessary to know whether one is at the centre or on the circumference? Provided that entirely consecrated to Thee, living only for Thee and by Thee, I carry out better and better the task Thou givest me, all the rest has no importance at all. I would say more: provided Thy work is accomplished in the world as well and as completely as it can be, does it matter which individual or group realises this work?

O my sweet Master, in peace, serenity, equanimity, I give myself to Thee and merge in Thee, my thought calm and tranquil, my heart smiling; Thy work will be done, I know, and Thy victory is certain.

O my sweet Master, grant to all the sovereign boon of Thy illumination!

May 15, 1914

AS on reaching a summit, one discovers a vast horizon, so, O Lord, when one's consciousness is identified with that intermediate domain between Thy Unity and the manifested world, one participates both in Thy Infinitude and in the realisation of the world. It is as though one were at a centre where the consciousness, wholly steeped in Thy effective Power, could direct the ray of Thy forces upon the lowly instrument moving among its brother instruments. From the height of these transcendent regions the unity of physical substance is clearly visible, and yet the body which serves as a particular instrument in the material field seems specially precise and distinct like a stronger point amidst this whole, at once multiple and one, in which the forces circulate evenly.

This perception has not left me since yesterday. It has settled in as something definitive, and all the outer activity which apparently continues as usual, has become mechanical like a marvellously articulated and animated toy moved by the consciousness from the height of its seat which though no longer individual is still universal, that is, which is not yet completely merged in Thy Oneness. All the laws of individual manifestation have become clear to me, but in so synthetical, so global, so simultaneous a way, that it is impossible to express this in our ordinary language.

May 16, 1914

I WAS interrupted yesterday just when I was trying to formulate the experience I had. And now everything seems changed. That precise knowledge, that clear-sightedness has given place to a great love for Thee, O Lord, which has seized my whole being from the outer organism to the deepest consciousness, and all lies prostrate at Thy feet in an ardent aspiration for a definitive identification with Thee, an absorption in Thee. I implored Thee with all the energy I could summon. And once again, just when it seemed to me that my consciousness was going to disappear in Thine, just when all my being was nothing but a pure crystal reflecting Thy Presence, someone came and interrupted my concentration.

Such is, indeed, the symbol of the existence Thou givest me as my share, in which outer usefulness, the work for all, holds a much greater place even than the supreme realisation. All the circumstances of my life seem always to tell me on Thy behalf: "It is not through supreme concentration that thou wilt realise oneness, it is by spreading out in all." May Thy will be done, O Lord.

Now I understand clearly that union with Thee is not an aim to be pursued, so far as this present individuality is concerned; it is an accomplished fact since a long time. And that is why Thou seemest to tell me always: "Do not delight in the ecstatic contemplation of this union; accomplish the mission I have entrusted to thee upon earth."

And the individual work to be carried on simultaneously with the collective work is to become aware and take possession of all the activities and parts of the being, the definitive establishment of consciousness in the highest point, making possible both the prescribed action and the constant communion with Thee. The joys of perfect union cannot come until what has to be done is done.

First, union must be preached to all, afterwards work; but for those who have realised the union, every moment of their life must be an integral expression of Thy will through them.

May 17, 1914

O LORD, deliver me from the mental influences which weigh upon me, so that, completely free, I may soar towards Thee.

O Thou, Universal Being, Supreme Unity in perceptible form, through an irresistible aspiration I nestled within Thy heart, then I was Thy heart itself, and I knew then that Thy heart is no other than the Child who plays and creates the worlds. Thou didst tell me, "One day thou wilt be my head but for the moment turn thy gaze towards the earth." And on the earth now I am the joyful child who plays.

These were the two sentences I wrote yesterday by a kind of absolute necessity. The first, as though the power of the prayer would not be complete unless it were traced on paper. The second, as though the stability of the experience could not be had unless I unburdened my mind of it by noting it down in writing.

May 18, 1914

THOU art the sole Reality, O Lord, Thou art Omnipotence and Eternity. And he who is united with Thee in the depths of his being becomes Thy Reality in its eternal and immutable omnipotence. But for others the command is, even while remaining in contact with Thee, to turn their eyes and activity towards the earth; such is the mission Thou hast given them. Here begins the difficulty, for everything depends upon the perfection of the various states of their being and, even after attaining the sublime identification, they must still work at perfecting the instrument which will manifest Thy divine Will. This is where the task becomes arduous. Everything seems to me mediocre, insufficient, neutral, almost inert in the present instrument which Thou makest me call "myself"; and the more I am united with Thee, the more do I realise the mediocrity of its faculties and its manifestation. Everything in it seems to me an incorrigible approximation. And if that cannot disturb me in any way, it is because the true self is lying at Thy feet or nestling in Thy heart or conscious with Thy eternal and immutable Consciousness, and looks at the whole manifestation with a smile of patient and understanding benevolence.

May 19, 1914

THIS mental being which throughout my individual existence had the power to set all my faculties working: deep devotion for Thee, infinite compassion for men, ardent aspiration for knowledge, effort for self-perfection — seems to have fallen into a deep sleep and no longer sets anything at all in movement. All the individual faculties slumber and the consciousness is not yet fully awake in the transcendent states; that is, its wakefulness in them is intermittent and in between there is sleep. Something in this being aspires for solitude and absolute silence for a little while, so as to come out of this unsatisfactory transition; and something else knows that it is Thy will that this instrument be consecrated to the service of all, even if this must apparently be harmful to its self-perfecting.

Something in this being tells Thee, O Lord:
"I know nothing,
I am nothing,
I can do nothing,
I am in the darkness of inconscience."

And something else knows that it is Thyself and thus the supreme perfection.

What is going to come out of that? How will such a state come to an end? Whether it is inertia or true patience, I do not know; but without haste or desire I lie at Thy feet and wait. . . .

147

May 20, 1914

FROM the height of that summit which is the identification with Thy divine infinite Love, Thou didst turn my eyes to this complex body which has to serve Thee as Thy instrument. And Thou didst tell me, "It is myself; dost thou not see my light shining in it?" And indeed I saw Thy divine Love, clothed in intelligence, then in strength, constituting this body in its smallest cells and shining so brightly in it that it was nothing but a combination of millions of radiant sparks, all manifesting that they were Thyself.

And now all darkness has disappeared, and Thou alone livest, in different worlds, in different forms but with an identical life, immutable and eternal.

This divine world of Thy immutable domain of pure love and indivisible unity must be brought into close communion with the divine world of all the other domains, right down to the most material in which Thou art the centre and very constitution of each atom. To establish a bond of perfect consciousness between all these successive divine worlds is the only way to live constantly, invariably in Thee, accomplishing integrally the mission Thou hast entrusted to the entire being in all its states of consciousness and all its modes of activity.

O my sweet Master, Thou hast caused a new veil to be rent, another veil of my ignorance and, without leaving my blissful place in Thy eternal heart, I am at the same time in the imperceptible but infinite heart of each of the atoms constituting my body.

Strengthen this complete and perfect consciousness. Make me enter into all the details of its perfection and grant that, without leaving Thee for a single moment, I may constantly move up and down this infinite ladder, according to the necessity of the work Thou hast prescribed for me.

I am Thine, I am in Thee, Thyself, in the plenitude of eternal bliss.

May 21, 1914*

OUTSIDE all manifestation, in the immutable silence of Eternity, I am in Thee, O Lord, an unmoving beatitude. In that which, out of Thy puissance and marvellous light, forms the centre and reality of the atoms of matter I find Thee; thus without going out of Thy Presence I can disappear in Thy supreme consciousness or see Thee in the radiant particles of my being. And for the moment that is the plenitude of Thy life and Thy illumination.

I see Thee, I am Thyself, and between these two poles my intense love aspires towards Thee.

May 22, 1914 *

WHEN we have discerned successively what is real from what is unreal in all the states of being and all the worlds of life, when we have arrived at the perfect and integral certitude of the sole Reality, we must turn our gaze from the heights of this supreme consciousness towards the individual aggregate which serves as the immediate instrument for Thy manifestation upon earth, and see in it nothing but Thee, our sole real existence. Thus each atom of this aggregate will be awakened to receive Thy sublime influence; the ignorance and the darkness will disappear not only from the central consciousness of the being but also from its most external mode of expression. It is only by the fulfilment, by the perfection of this labour of transfiguration that there can be manifested the plenitude of Thy Presence, Thy Light and Thy Love.

Lord, Thou makest me understand this truth ever more clearly; lead me step by step on that path. My whole being down to its smallest atom aspires for the perfect knowledge of Thy presence and a complete union with it. Let every obstacle disappear, let Thy divine knowledge replace in every part the darkness of the ignorance. Even as Thou hast illumined the central consciousness, the will in the being, enlighten too this outermost substance. And let the whole individuality, from its first origin and essence to its last projection and most material body, be unified in a perfect realisation and a complete manifestation of Thy sole Reality.

151

Nothing is in the universe but Thy Life, Thy Light, Thy Love.

Let everything become resplendent and transfigured by the knowledge of Thy Truth.

Thy divine love floods my being; Thy supreme light is shining in every cell; all exults because it knows Thee and because it is one with Thee.

May 23, 1914

O LORD, Thou of whom I would be constantly conscious and whom I would realise in the smallest cells of
my being, Thou whom I would know as myself and see
manifested in all things, Thou who art the sole reality,
the sole cause and aim of existence, grant that my love
for Thee may grow ever greater so that I may be all
love, Thy love itself, and that, being Thy love, I may
unite integrally with Thee. May this love grow more
and more intense, complete, luminous, powerful; may
this love become an irresistible urge towards Thee, the
invincible means of manifesting Thee. May everything in
this being become pure, profound, disinterested, divine
love — from the unfathomable depths to the outermost
substance. May the God with form who manifests in this
aggregate be entirely moulded from Thy complete and
sublime love, the love which is at once the source and the
realisation of all knowledge; may thought be clarified,
organised, enlightened, transformed by Thy love; may
all the life-forces, solely impregnated by Thy love and
moulded from it, draw from it irresistible purity and constant energy, power and rectitude. May this weakened
intermediary being, take advantage of its weakness to
reconstitute itself with elements entirely moulded from
Thy love, and may this body, now a burning brazier,
radiate Thy divine, impersonal, sublime and calm love
from every pore. . . . May the brain be reconstituted by
Thy love. Lastly, may Thy love overflow, flood, penetrate, transfigure, regenerate, animate all things, with the

power, the splendour, the sweetness and force which are its very own. In Thy love is peace, in Thy love is joy, in Thy love is Thy servitor's sovereign lever of work.

Thy love is vaster than the universe and more lasting than all the ages; it is infinite, eternal, it is Thyself. And it is Thyself I want to be and that I am, for such is Thy law, such is Thy will.

May 24, 1914

O MY sweet Master, let me not be submerged by outer things. They have no interest, no savour for me. If I busy myself with them, it is because I feel that such is Thy will and the work must be accomplished integrally, down to the least details of the action and substance. But it is quite enough to turn one's attention to them and infuse Thy forces into them as much as possible. They must not be allowed to take precedence of the true realities in one's consciousness.

O my sweet Master, I aspire for Thee, for the knowledge of what Thou art, for identification with Thee. I ask for a greater love, growing always purer, always vaster, always more intense and I find myself as it were submerged in Matter; is this Thy reply? As Thou hast Thyself accepted to be thus submerged in Matter so as to awaken it gradually to consciousness, is this the result of a more perfect identification with Thee? Is this not Thy answer to me: "If thou wouldst learn to love truly, this is how thou shouldst love . . ." . . . in darkness and unconsciousness?

O my Lord, my sweet Master, Thou knowest that I belong to Thee and that always I want what Thou willest; but do not let any doubt about what Thou willest arise in me. Enlighten me in some way in the immutable peace of the heart. Let me be submerged in darkness if that is necessary, but at least let me know that it is Thou who willest it.

Lord, in response, I hear singing within my heart the hymn of gladness of Thy divine and permanent Presence.

May 25, 1914

O DIVINE Master of love and purity, grant that in its least stages, its smallest activities, this instrument which wants to serve Thee worthily may be purified of all egoism, all error, all obscurity, so that nothing in it may impair, deform or stop Thy action. How many little recesses lie yet in shadow, far from the full light of Thy illumination: for these I ask the supreme happiness of this illumination.

Oh, to be the pure flawless crystal which lets Thy divine ray pass without obscuring, colouring or distorting it! — not from a desire for perfection but so that Thy work may be done as perfectly as possible.

And when I ask Thee this, the "I" which speaks to Thee is the entire Earth, aspiring to be this pure diamond, a perfect reflector of Thy supreme light. All the hearts of men beat within my heart, all their thoughts vibrate in my thought, the slightest aspiration of a docile animal or a modest plant unites with my formidable aspiration, and all this rises towards Thee, for the conquest of Thy love and light, scaling the summits of Being to attain Thee, ravish Thee from Thy motionless beatitude and make Thee penetrate the darkness of suffering to transform it into divine Joy, into sovereign Peace. And this violence is made of an infinite love which gives itself and a trustful serenity which smiles with the certitude of Thy perfect Unity.

O my sweet Master, Thou art the Triumpher and the Triumph, the Victor and the Victory!

May 26, 1914 *

ON the surface is the storm, the sea is in turmoil, waves clash and leap one on another and break with a mighty uproar. But all the time, under this water in fury, are vast smiling expanses, peaceful and motionless. They look upon the surface agitation as an indispensable act; for matter has to be vigorously churned if it is to become capable of manifesting entirely the divine light. Behind the troubled appearance, behind the struggle and anguish of the conflict, the consciousness remains firm at its post; observing all the movements of the outer being, it intervenes only to rectify direction and position, so as not to allow the play to become too dramatic. This intervention is now firm and a little severe, now ironical, a call to order or a mockery, full always of a strong, gentle, peaceful and smiling benevolence.

In the silence I beheld Thy infinite and eternal Beatitude.

Then softly a prayer rises towards Thee from what is still in the shadow and the struggle: O sweet Master, O supreme Giver of illumination and purity, grant that all substance and every activity may be no more anything other than a constant manifestation of Thy divine Love and Thy sovereign Serenity. . . .

And in my heart is the song of gladness of Thy sublime magnificence.

May 27, 1914

IN each one of the domains of the being, the consciousness must be awakened to the perfect existence, knowledge and bliss. These three worlds or modes of the Divine are found in the physical reality as well as in the states of force and light and those of impersonality and infinitude, of eternity. When one enters with full consciousness into the higher states, to live this existence, light and bliss is easy, almost inevitable. But what is very important, as well as very difficult, is to awaken the being to this triple divine consciousness in the most material worlds. This is the first point. Then one must succeed in finding the centre of all the divine worlds (probably in the intermediate world), whence one can unite the consciousness of these divine worlds, synthetise them, and act simultaneously and with full awareness in all domains.

I know that it is a very long way from these incomplete and imperfect explanations to the sublime reality which manifests Thee, O Lord. Thy splendour, Thy power and Thy magnificence, Thy incommensurable love are above all explanation and comment. But my intellect needs to represent things to itself at least a little schematically, in order to allow the most material states of the being to enter as completely as possible into harmony with Thy Will.

Yet it is in the deep silence of my mute and total adoration that I best understand Thee. For then who can say what loves, what is loved, and what is the power of loving in itself? All three are but one in an infinite bliss.

O give to everyone, Lord, the boon of that incomparable bliss.

May 28, 1914

THOU settest in motion, Thou stirrest and churnest the innumerable elements of this world, so that, from their primal darkness, their primeval chaos, they may awaken to consciousness and the full light of knowledge. And Thou usest Thy supreme love to churn all these elements in this way. And it is from Thy infinite, unfathomable heart that these inexhaustible torrents of love spring forth. Thy heart is my dwelling-place, Thy heart is the reality of my being. In Thy heart I have nestled and I have become Thy heart.

Peace, peace upon all beings.

May 29, 1914

O MY sweet Lord, those who are in Thy head, that is, to speak more intellectually, those who have identified their consciousness with the absolute Consciousness, those who have become Thy supreme Knowledge, can no longer have any love for Thee, since they are Thyself. They enjoy that infinite bliss characteristic of all awareness of Thy supreme Essence, but the devotion of the adorer who turns with ecstasy to that which is higher and above him can no longer exist. So, to him whose mission upon earth is to manifest Thy love, Thou teachest to have this pure and infinite love for all the manifested universe; the love which at first was made of adoration and admiration is transformed into a love all made of compassion and devotedness.

Oh, the divine splendour of Thy eternal Unity!
Oh, the infinite sweetness of Thy Beatitude!
Oh, the sovereign majesty of Thy Knowledge!
Thou art the Inconceivable, the Marvellous One!

161

May 31, 1914

WHEN the sun set in the indrawn contemplation of the calm twilight, all my being prostrated itself before Thee, O Lord, in mute adoration and complete self-giving. Then I was the whole earth and the whole earth prostrated itself before Thee, imploring the benediction of Thy illumination, the beatitude of Thy love. Oh, the kneeling earth that supplicates to Thee, then is ingathered in the silence of the night, waiting in both patience and anxiety for the illumination so ardently desired. If there is a sweetness in being Thy divine love at work in the world, there is as great a sweetness in being the infinite aspiration which rises towards that infinite love. And to be able to change thus, to be successively, almost simultaneously, what receives and what gives, what transfigures and what is transfigured, to be identified with the painful darkness as with the all-powerful splendour and, in this double identification, to discover the secret of Thy sovereign unity, is this not a way of expressing, of accomplishing Thy supreme will? . . .

O my sweet Master, my heart is a flaming chapel, and Thou art seated there permanently like the sublimest of idols; so it is that Thy form appears to me, clothed in magnificence, in the midst of the flames consuming my heart for Thee, and at the same time, in my head, I see Thee, know Thee as the Inconceivable, the Unknowable, the Formless; and in this double perception, this double knowledge, lies the plenitude of contentment.

June 1, 1914

O VICTORIOUS power of divine Love, Thou art the sovereign Master of this universe, Thou art its creator and its saviour, Thou hast permitted it to emerge from chaos, and now Thou leadest it to its eternal goal.

There is not a thing so humble but in it I see Thee resplendent, not a being apparently so hostile to Thy will but I feel Thee live in it and act and radiate.

O my sweet Master, essence of this love, I am Thy heart, and the torrents of Thy love pass through the entirety of my being and flow out to awaken Thy love in all things or rather to awaken all things to the consciousness of Thy love which animates all.

All those who do not recognise Thee, all those who do not know Thee, all those who try to turn away from Thy sweet and divine law, I take into my arms of love, I cradle them in my heart of love and offer them to Thy divine flames, so that penetrated by Thy miraculous effluence, they may be converted in Thy beatitude.

O Love, resplendent Love, Thou penetratest, Thou transfigurest all.

June 2, 1914

IN a silent contemplation, in a mute adoration, uniting myself with all this dark and painful substance, I hail Thee, O Lord, as the divine saviour; I bless Thy love as the supreme liberator, I offer thanks for its countless boons, and I give myself fully to Thee so that Thou mayst complete Thy work of perfectioning. Then identifying myself with Thy love, I am nothing but Thy inexhaustible love; I penetrate all things; living within the heart of each atom I kindle therein the fire which purifies and transfigures, the fire that never burns out, the messenger flame of Thy beatitudes, realiser of all perfections.

Then this very love grows silently contemplative, and turning to Thee, O unknowable Splendour, awaits in ecstasy Thy New Manifestation . . .

June 3, 1914

NOW that the whole being is more and more deeply plunged into material activity, into the physical realisation which includes such a multitude of details to be thought of and regulated, I call to Thee, O Lord, so that my consciousness, turned thus outwards, may constantly keep this communion with Thee, which is the source of all peace, all strength, all bliss.

O my sweet Master, accomplish all the work Thyself through this individual being in its integrality. Or rather, do not let anything in this individual being forget at any moment that it is only an instrument, an illusion made real for Thy intervention in it, and that Thou alone art and actest.

Oh, the benediction of Thy immutable Presence . . .

June 4, 1914

O THOU who triumphest over all obstacles, Thou shalt be in us the victory over all that would be an obstacle to the accomplishment of Thy divine law. Thou wilt dispel the darkness of ignorance and the black smoke of egoistic ill-will; Thou wilt dissolve all wrong suggestions and strengthen in us a pure and clear vision and the perspicacity which does not let itself be deceived by disruptive thoughts and conflicting wills for disorder.

O my sweet Master, Thy infinite love is the reality of our being; who can struggle against its all-powerful action? It penetrates everything, it passes through every obstacle, whether it be the inertia of a heavy ignorance or the resistance of an uncomprehending ill-will. O my sweet Master, through and by this love, Thou shinest resplendent in all things, and this splendour of Thine, ever-increasing in its force, shall radiate its action over all the earth and become perceptible to every consciousness.

Who can resist Thy divine power?

Thou art the sole and supreme Reality.

My being is ingathered in a mute adoration and everything disappears that is not Thou.

June 9, 1914

LORD, I am before Thee like an offering aflame in the blazing fire of the divine union. . . .

And what is thus before Thee is all the stones of this house and all it contains, all those who cross its threshold and all who see it, all who are connected with it in any way and from one to another the whole earth.

From this centre, this burning hearth which is now and shall be more and more permeated with Thy light and with Thy love, Thy forces will radiate over all the earth, visibly and invisibly in the hearts of all and in their thoughts . . .

Such is the assurance Thou givest me in answer to my aspiration for Thee.

An immense wave of love descends over all things and penetrates all things.

Peace, peace upon all the earth, victory, plenitude, wonder . . .

O beloved children, unhappy and ignorant, O thou, rebellious and violent Nature, open your hearts, calm your forces, for here comes the sweet omnipotence of Love, here is the pure radiance of the light that penetrates you. This human hour, this earthly hour is beautiful over all other hours. Let each and all know it and rejoice in the plenitude that is given.

O sorrowful hearts and careworn brows, foolish obscurity and ignorant ill-will, let your anguish be calmed and effaced.

Lo, the splendour of the new word arrives: *"Here am I."*

June 11, 1914

EVERY morning, O Lord, an innumerable salutation rises towards Thee, a salutation from all the states of being and from all the multitude of their elements. And it is a daily consecration of all things to the All, a call from ignorance and egoism to Thy light and love. And Thy answer comes constant and is integrally perceived: All is light, all is love, ignorance and egoism are but vain phantoms, they can be dissolved.

And over all things spreads Thy sovereign peace, Thy fecund calmness.

June 12, 1914

O MY sweet Master, eternal splendour, I can only unite with Thee in silence and peace, saying that Thy Will may be done in every detail as in the whole. Take possession of Thy kingdom, master all that revolts against Thee, heal the souls who do not know Thee and the intellects that do not want to submit and be consecrated to Thee. Awaken our slumbering energies, stimulate our courage, enlighten us, O Lord, show us the Way.

My heart is overflowing with a sovereign peace, my thought is calm and silent.

At the core of all that is, of all that will be, of all that is not, is Thy divine and unchanging smile.

June 13, 1914

FIRST of all, knowledge must be conquered, that is, one must learn to know Thee, to be united with Thee, and all means are good and may be used to attain this goal. But it would be a great mistake to believe that all is done when this goal is attained. All is done in principle, the victory is gained in theory, and those whose motive is only an egoistic aspiration for their own salvation may feel satisfied and live only in and for this communion, without caring at all for Thy manifestation.

But those whom Thou hast appointed as Thy representatives upon earth cannot rest content with the result so obtained. To know Thee first and before all else, yes; but once Thy knowledge is acquired there remains all the work of Thy manifestation; and then there intervene the quality, force, complexity and perfection of this manifestation. Very often those who have known Thee, dazzled and rapt in ecstasy by this knowledge, have been content to see Thee for themselves and express Thee somehow or other in their outermost being. He who wants to be perfect in Thy manifestation cannot be satisfied with that; he must manifest Thee on all the planes, in all the states of being and thus turn the knowledge he has acquired to the best account for the whole universe.

Before the immensity of this programme, the entire being exults and sings a hymn of gladness to Thee.

All nature in full conscious activity, all vibrant with Thy sovereign forces, responds to their inspiration and wants to be illumined and transfigured by them . . . Thou art the Master of the world, the sole Reality.

June 14, 1914

I T is a veritable work of creation we have to do: to create activities, new modes of being so that this Force, unknown to the earth till today, may manifest in its plenitude. To this travail I am consecrated, O Lord, for this is what Thou wantest of me. But since Thou hast appointed me for this work, Thou must give me the means, that is, the knowledge necessary for its realisation. We shall unite our efforts: the entire individual being will concentrate in a constant call for the knowledge of the mode of manifestation of this Force, and Thou, supreme centre of the being, Thou wilt emanate the Force fully so that it may penetrate, transfigure and overcome all obstacles. It is a pact Thou hast signed with the worlds of individual life. Thou hast made a promise, Thou hast sent into these worlds those who can and that which can fulfil this promise. This now demands Thy integral help so that what has been promised may be realised.

In us must take place the union of the two wills and two currents, so that from their contact may spring forth the illuminating spark.

And since this *must* be done, *this will be done*.

June 15, 1914

"LIE cradled in my heart and do not worry: what has to be done will be done. And it is just when thou doest it unknowingly that it is done best" . . .

I am in Thy heart, Lord, and nothing can take me away from it. And it is from the unfathomable depths of this heart, in the smiling peace of its beatitude, that I look at all the outer forms of Thy manifestation struggling and endeavouring to understand Thee better, manifest Thee better.

If the hour has come, as Thou lettest me know, for the new forms of Thy realisation, these forms will inevitably be born. Something in the being senses it but does not yet know; so it makes an effort to adapt itself, to prove equal to what Thou askest of it. But what is conscious of Thee and lives in Thy force knows that this new form is only an infinitesimal progress in the infinite progression of Thy manifestation, and looks at every form with the serenity of eternal plenitude.

And in this serenity is the very omnipotence of realisation.

One must know how to soar in an immutable confidence; in the sure flight is perfect knowledge.

June 16, 1914

LIKE a sun Thy splendour descends upon the earth and Thy rays will illumine the world. All those elements which are pure enough, plastic enough, sufficiently receptive to manifest the very splendour of the central fire-nucleus are grouping themselves together. This grouping is not arbitrary and does not depend on the will or aspiration of one element or another, it depends on what it is, it is independent of any individual decision. Thy splendour wants to radiate; what is capable of manifesting it manifests it, and these elements gather together to reconstitute as perfectly as possible in this world of division the divine Centre which has to be manifested.

In the wonder of this contemplation all the cells of the being exult; and, seeing That which Is, the integral substance passes into an ecstasy. How can this substance be now distinguished from Thyself? It is Thou — completely, entirely, intensely — in a perfect identification, Thou.

June 17, 1914

ALL that has been conceived and realised so far is mediocre, banal, insufficient beside what ought to be. The perfections of the past no longer have any force now. A new puissance is needed to transform the new powers and to subject them to Thy divine will. "Ask and this shall be", is Thy constant answer. And now, O Lord, Thou must create in this being a constant aspiration, uninterrupted, intense, passionate, in an immutable serenity. Silence, peace are there: there must also be the persistence of the intensity. Oh, Thy heart sings a hallelujah of gladness as if what Thou willest were on the way to its fulfilment. . . . Destroy all these elements, that from their ashes may emerge new elements adapted to the new manifestation.

Oh, the immensity of Thy luminous Peace!

Oh, the omnipotence of Thy sovereign Love!

And beyond all that we can imagine, the ineffable splendour of what we feel to be coming. Give us the Thought, give us the Word, give us the Force.

Enter the arena of the world, O new-born Unknown One!

June 18, 1914

ALWAYS the same Will is at work. The Force is there awaiting the possibility to manifest: we must discover the new form which will make the new manifestation possible. And Thou, only Thou, O Lord, can grant us this knowledge. It is for us with our whole being to make the effort, to ask, to aspire. But it is for Thee to answer with the Illumination, the Knowledge and the Power.

Oh, the canticle of joy of Thy victorious Presence . . .

June 19, 1914

FILL our hearts with the delight of Thy love. Flood our minds with the splendour of Thy light. Grant that we may effectuate Thy Victory!

June 20, 1914

THOU must accomplish the work of transfiguration, Thou must teach us the path to be followed and Thou must give us the power to follow it to the very end. . . .

O Thou source of all love and all light, Thou whom we cannot know in Thyself but can manifest ever more completely and perfectly, Thou whom we cannot conceive but can approach in profound silence, to complete Thy incommensurable boons Thou must come to our help until we have gained Thy victory. . . .

Let that true love be born which soothes all suffering; establish that immutable peace wherein resides true power; give us the sovereign knowledge which dispels all darkness. . . .

From the infinite depths to this most external body, in its smallest elements, Thou dost move and live and vibrate and set all in motion, and the whole being is now only a single block, infinitely multiple yet absolutely coherent, animated by one tremendous vibration: Thou.

June 21, 1914

To be at once a passive and perfectly pure mirror, turned simultaneously without and within, to the results of the manifestation and the sources of this manifestation, so that the consequences may be placed before the guiding will, and to be also the realising activity of that will, this, more or less, is what a human being ought to be. . . . To combine these two attitudes of passive receptivity and realising activity is precisely the most difficult of all things. And that is what Thou expectest of us, O Lord, and as Thou dost expect it of us, there is no doubt that Thou wilt give us the means of realising it.

For what must be will be, more splendidly yet than we can imagine.

Oh, may Thy love grow wider and wider in the manifestation, ever more sublime, ever deeper, ever vaster. . . .

June 22, 1914

WHAT has to be will be, what has to be done will be done. . . .

What a calm assurance Thou hast put into my being, O Lord. Who or what will manifest Thee? Who can say it yet? . . . In all things that strive towards a new, ever higher and completer expression, Thou art present. But the centre of the light is still not manifested, for the centre of manifestation is not yet perfectly adapted.

O divine Master, that which has to be will be and it will perhaps be very different from what all expect. . . .

But how is it possible to express certain silent secrets? The force is here; in it is the self.

When and how will this force spring forth? When Thou findest the instrument ready.

Oh, the sweetness of Thy calm assurance, the power of Thy Peace! . . .

June 23, 1914

THOU art the sovereign power of transformation, why shouldst Thou not act on all who are brought into contact with Thee through our mediation? We lack faith in Thy power: always we think that men should in their conscious thought want this integral transformation for it to come about; we forget that it is Thou who willest in them and that Thou canst will in such a way that all their being is illumined by it. . . . We doubt Thy power, O Lord, and thus become bad intermediaries for it and veil the major part of its transforming force.

Oh, give us the faith which we lack; give us the certitude of detail which is wanting in us. Deliver us from the ordinary way of thinking and judging; grant that we may live in the consciousness of Thy infinite love and see it at work at every moment and that by our consciousness of it we may bring it into touch with the most material states of being. . . .

O Lord, deliver us from all ignorance, give us true faith.

June 24, 1914

FROM the point of view of the manifestation, the work to be carried forward upon earth, a hierarchy is needed — but in this world which is still in disorder, can it be established unarbitrarily, that is, in perfect conformity with Thy law? . . . The witness being, calm, indifferent, smiling, looks upon the play, the comedy which is unfolding itself, and awaits circumstances with serenity, knowing that they are nothing but a very imperfect translation of what should be.

But the religious being turns to Thee, O Lord, in a great aspiration of love, and implores Thy help so that it may be *the best* that shall be realised, so that as many obstacles as possible may be overcome, all possible obscurities dispelled, all possible egoistic ill-will vanquished. It is not *the best* possible in circumstances of the present disorder which must happen — for that always happens — it is these circumstances themselves which, through a greater effort than ever yet was made, must be transfigured, so that a "best", new in quality, new in quantity, an altogether exceptional "best" may be manifested.

So let it be.

*

It is always wrong to want to evaluate the future or even to foresee it by the thought we have about it, for this thought is the present, it is in its very impersonality the translation of present relations which are necessarily not the future relations between all the elements of the terrestrial problem. Deducing future circumstances from present ones is a mental activity of the nature of reasoning, even if the deduction takes place in the subconscient and is translated in the being into the form of intuition; but reasoning is a human faculty, that is, it is individual; its inspirations do not come from the infinite, the unlimited, the Divine. It is only in the Omniscience, only when one is at once What knows, what is to be known and the power of knowing that one can become conscious of all relations, past, present and future; but in this state there is no longer a past, present or future, *all is* eternally. The order of manifestation of all these relations does not solely depend upon the supreme impulsion, the divine Law, it depends also upon the resistance put up against this law by the most external world; from the combination of the two there comes forth the manifestation and so far as it is at present possible for me to know, this combination is in a way undetermined. This is what makes the play, the unexpectedness of the play.

184

June 25, 1914

WHAT wisdom is there in wanting to be like this or like that? Why torment oneself thus? Art Thou not the supreme worker? Is it not our duty to be Thy docile instruments and, when Thou puttest the instrument aside for a time, will it complain that Thou abandonest it because Thou dost not make it work? Will it not be able to enjoy calm and repose after having enjoyed activity and struggle?

One must be always vigilant, attentive to the least call, so as not to be asleep or inert when Thou givest the signal for action, whether with the mind, the feelings or the body; but one must not confuse this constant state of expectation and devoted goodwill with an anxious and uneasy agitation, a fear of not being this or that and of displeasing Thee, that is, of not conforming with what Thou expectest of us.

Thy heart is the supreme shelter, that wherein all care is soothed. Oh, leave it wide open, this heart, so that all those who are tormented may find there a sovereign refuge! . . .

Pierce this darkness, let light flash forth;
Still this tumult, establish peace;
Calm this violence, let love reign;
Become the warrior, triumphant over obstacles;
Win the victory.

June 26, 1914

HAIL to Thee, O Lord, Master of the world. Give us the power to do the work without being attached to it and to develop the capacities of individual manifestation without living in the illusion of personality. Strengthen our vision of reality; make firm our perception of unity; deliver us from all ignorance, all darkness.

We do not ask for the perfection of the instrument, knowing that in the world of relativities all perfection is relative: this instrument, fashioned for action in this world, must, in order to be able to act, belong to this world; but the consciousness that animates it should be identified with Thine, it should be the universal and eternal consciousness animating the varied multitude of bodies.

O Lord, grant that we may rise above the ordinary forms of manifestation so that Thou mayst find the tools necessary for Thy new manifestation.

Do not let us lose sight of the goal; grant that we may always be united with Thy force, the force which the earth does not yet know and which Thou hast given us the mission to reveal to it.

In a deep meditation, all the states of manifestation consecrate themselves to Thy manifestation.

June 27, 1914

MY being is happy with what Thou givest it; what Thou wantest from it, it will do, without weakness, without vain modesty and without futile ambition. What does it matter which place one occupies, what mission Thou entrustest? . . . Does not all lie in the fact of being entirely Thine, as perfectly as one can be, without the least care of any kind?

In this deep and steadfast confidence that Thy work will be done and that Thou hast created and appointed those who have to accomplish it, why strain one's energy uselessly and want what is already realised? Thou hast given me, O Lord, the sovereign peace of this confidence; Thou hast granted me the incomparable boon of living in Thy love, by Thy love, of being Thy love ever more and more; and in this love is complete and unchanging beatitude.

I address but one prayer to Thee, which l know to be granted in advance: Always increase the number of elements, atoms or universes, capable of living integrally in and by Thy love.

Peace, peace upon all the earth. . . .

June 28, 1914

ALL Nature hails Thee, O Lord, and with arms lifted and hands outstretched she implores Thee. Not that she doubts Thy infinite generosity and thinks she must ask in order to have; but that is her way of bowing to Thee and giving herself to Thee, for is this giving anything else than being ready to receive? She delights in thus offering a prayer to Thee though she knows that this prayer is superfluous. But it is an ardent and happy adoration. And the feeling of devotion is thus satisfied without in any way hurting the intellectual consciousness which knows Thee to be one with everything and present in everything.

But all the veils must vanish and the light become complete in all hearts.

O Lord, in spite of the work, in it, give us that perfect calm of the spirit which makes possible the divine identification, the integral knowledge.

My love for Thee, O Lord, is Thyself and yet my love bows down before Thee in deep devotion.

June 29, 1914

GIVE joy, peace and happiness to them all. . . . If they suffer, illumine their suffering and make it a means of transfiguration; grant them the beatitude of Thy love and the peace of Thy unity; may their hearts feel vibrating within them Thy eternal Presence. They are all in me, O Lord, I am in them all, and since instead of an "I", there is now only Thy sovereign love, they are all in Thy love and will be transfigured by it.

O Lord, my sweet Master, unknowable splendour, give them joy, peace, beatitude.

June 30, 1914

EACH activity in its own field accomplishing its particular mission, without disorder, without confusion, one enveloping the other, and all graded hierarchically around a single centre: Thy will. . . . What is most lacking in all beings is clarity and order; each element, each state of being, instead of fulfilling its function in harmony with all the others, wants to be the whole in itself, perfectly autonomous and independent. And there lies the ignorant error of all the universe, a global error repeated in millions and millions of forms. But under the pretext that these activities are separate and in disorder, to want to suppress them so as to let only Thy single Will subsist, which in its solitude would no longer have any reason to exist, would be an undertaking as absurd as it is unrealisable. It is easier, indeed, to suppress than to organise; but harmonious order is a realisation far superior to suppression. And even if the final aim were a return to Non-Being, the return would seem possible to me only through a highest perfection of the being. . . .

O my sweet Master, grant to them that they may feel Thy infinite tenderness and in the calm repose that it brings, be able to see and realise the supreme order of Thy law.

Let Thy will which is all love manifest, let Thy peace manifest.

July 1, 1914

W E hail Thee, O Lord, with adoration and with joy, and give ourselves to Thee in a gift constantly renewed, so that Thy will may be accomplished upon earth and in all the places of this universe.

When we turn towards Thee the thought is mute but the heart exults; for Thou shinest resplendent in all things, and the least grain of sand may be an occasion for worship.

We bow down before Thee, we unite with Thee, O Lord, in a love that is limitless and full of an inexpressible beatitude.

Oh, grant this sovereign joy to all.

July 4, 1914

O SOVEREIGN Force, O victorious Power, Purity, Beauty, supreme Love, grant that this being in its integrality, this body in all its totality may draw near to Thee solemnly and offer to Thee in a complete and humble surrender this means of manifestation abandoned perfectly to Thy Will, if not perfectly ready for this realisation. . . .

With the calm and strong certitude that Thou wilt one day accomplish the expected miracle and manifest in its fullness Thy sublime splendour, we turn to Thee in a profound rapture, and silently implore Thee. . . .

Immensity, Infinitude, Wonder. . . . Thou alone art and Thou shinest resplendent in all things. The hour of Thy fulfilment is near. All Nature is ingathered in a solemn concentration.

Thou answerest her ardent call.

July 5, 1914

ALL that belongs to the outer, lower being which is still obscure, prostrates itself before Thee in a mute and fervent adoration, calling with all its strength Thy purifying action which will make it fit to manifest Thee fully.

And in this adoration is found perfect silence and perfect beatitude.

Thou repliest mercifully to the call: "What has to be done will be done. The necessary instruments will be prepared. Strive in the calm of certitude."

193

July 6, 1914

WHAT plenitude in the perception! The entire individual being, modest, humble, surrendered, adoring, calm and smiling, feeling one with all beings, unable to make any difference of value, in perfect solidarity with all things, is kneeling down before Thee together with them all; and at the same time the formidable omnipotence of *Thy Force which is here*, ready for the manifestation, waiting, building the propitious hour, the favourable opportunity: the incomparable splendour of Thy victorious sovereignty.

The Force is here. Rejoice, O you who are waiting and hoping: the new manifestation is sure, the new manifestation is at hand.

The Force is here.

All nature exults and sings in gladness, all nature is at a festival: *The Force is here.*

Arise and live; arise and be illuminated; arise and battle for the transfiguration of all:

The Force is here.

July 7, 1914

PEACE, peace upon all the earth. . . .

Not the peace of an inconscient sleep or a self-satisfied inertia; not the peace of a self-forgetful ignorance and a dark, heavy indifference, but the peace of the omnipotent force, the peace of perfect communion, the peace of integral awakening, of the disappearance of all limitation and all darkness. . . .

Why torment oneself and suffer, why this bitter struggle and painful revolt, why this vain violence, why this inconscient, heavy sleep? Awake without fear, appease your conflicts, silence your disputes, open your eyes and your hearts: the Force is there; it is there, divinely pure, luminous, powerful; it is there as a boundless love, a sovereign power, an indisputable reality, an unmixed peace, an uninterrupted beatitude, the Supreme Benediction; it is self-existence, the endless bliss of infinite knowledge . . . and it is something more which cannot yet be told, but which is already at work in the higher worlds beyond thought as the power of sovereign transfiguration, and also in the inconscient depths of Matter as the Irresistible Healer. . . .

Listen, listen, O thou who wouldst know.

Look, thou who wouldst see, contemplate and live:
The Force is here.

July 8, 1914

O DIVINE Force, supreme Illuminator, hearken to our prayer, move not away from us, do not withdraw, help us to fight the good fight, make firm our strength for the struggle, give us the force to conquer!

O my sweet Master, Thou whom I adore without being able to know Thee, Thou who I am without being able to realise Thee, my entire conscious individuality prostrates itself before Thee and implores, in the name of the workers in their struggle, and of the earth in her agony, in the name of suffering humanity and of striving Nature; O my sweet Master, O marvellous Unknowable, O Dispenser of all boons, Thou who makest light spring forth in the darkness and strength to arise out of weakness, support our effort, guide our steps, lead us to victory.

July 10, 1914

O THOU who eternally, immutably art, who consentest to Thy becoming in this world that Thou mayst bring into it a new Illumination, a new Impulsion, Thou art here, manifest Thyself more and more completely, always more perfectly; the instrument has given and gives itself to Thee with a fervent adhesion, a total surrender; Thou mayst reduce it to dust or transform it into a sun, it will resist nothing that is Thy Will. In this surrender lies its true strength and its true beatitude.

But why art Thou so considerate with the animality of the body? Is it because it must be given time to adapt itself to the marvellous complexity, the powerful infinity of Thy Force? Is it Thy Will that makes itself gentle and patient, is unwilling to precipitate things, leaves to the elements leisure to adapt themselves? . . . I mean — is it better thus or is it impossible otherwise? Is there here a particular incapacity which Thou dost tolerate with magnanimity or is this a general law which is an inevitable portion of all that has to be transformed? . . .

But it matters little what we think about it, since thus it is; the attitude alone is important: Should we fight, should we accept? And it is Thou who dictatest the attitude, it is Thy Will that determines it at each moment. Why foresee and contrive when it is enough to observe and to give a full adhesion?

The working in the constitution of the physical cells is perceptible: permeated with a considerable amount of

197

force they seem to expand and to become lighter. But the brain is still heavy and asleep. .... I unite myself to this body, O divine Master, and cry to Thee: Do not spare me, act with Thy sovereign omnipotence; for in me Thou hast put the will to an entire transfiguration.

July 11, 1914

THE entire physical being would like to be dissolved and reconstituted in an adoration that would have no bounds. O Lord, Thou who comest to touch Matter as the Messenger of the Supreme Power and Supreme Beatitude, Thou createst the conception of what the total realisation can be. And when the being believed it was definitively invested with Thy sublime mandate, Thou withdrawest, making it understand that it was only a promise, a token of what can be. Alas, what an imperfection in Matter it is that we cannot hold Thee! O Lord, use Thy omnipotence, work the miracle of Thy permanent Presence. . . . Why so much consideration? We must triumph or perish! . . .

Victory, victory, victory! We want the victory of Transfiguration!

July 12, 1914

IN all the states of being, in all the modes of activity, in all things, in all the worlds, one can meet Thee and unite with Thee, for Thou art everywhere and always present. He who has met Thee in one activity of his being or in one world of the universe, says "I have found Him" and seeks nothing more; he thinks he has reached the summit of human possibilities. What a mistake! In all the states, in all the modes, in all things, all worlds, all the elements we must discover Thee and unite with Thee and if one element is left aside, however small it may be, the communion cannot be perfect, the realisation cannot be accomplished.

And that is why to have found Thee is but a first step on an infinite ladder. . . .

O sweet Master, sovereign Transfigurator, put an end to all negligence, all lazy indolence, gather together all our energies, make them into an indomitable, irresistible will.

O Light, Love, ineffable Force, all the atoms cry to Thee so that Thou mayst penetrate and transfigure them. . . .

Give to all the supreme delight of the communion.

July 13, 1914

PATIENCE, strength, courage, calm and indomitable energy. . . .

Let the mind learn to be silent, let it not be eager to profit immediately by the forces which come to us from Thee for the integral manifestation. . . .

But why hast thou chosen for the expression of Thy Will the poorest element, the most mediocre, the most imperfect? . . .

July 15, 1914

WHAT, O Lord? . . .

Just as Thou wilt, just as Thou wilt. . . .

This instrument is weak, mediocre; Thou hast taught it that all activities are possible to it, that nothing was radically strange to it in all human activities; but it is in intensity, in perfection only that the Divine begins, and until now Thou hast not granted to it any extraordinary intensity, any real perfection. . . . Everything is in a state of promise, a promise not individual but collective; nothing is completely realised.

Why, O Lord?

Thou hast placed in my heart a peace so total that it seems to be almost indifference and in an immensity of calm serenity it says:

Just as Thou wilt, just as Thou wilt. . . .

July 16, 1914

SALUTATION of my silent and humble adoration. . . .
I bow down before Thy glory, for it dominates me
with all its splendour. . . .
Oh, let me dissolve at Thy feet, melt into Thee!

July 17, 1914

Earthly realisations easily take on a great importance in our eyes, for they are proportionate to our external being with this limited form which makes us men. But what is an earthly realisation beside Thee, before Thee? However perfect, complete, divine it may be, it is nothing but an indiscernible moment in Thy eternity; and the results obtained by it, however powerful and marvellous they may be, are nothing but an imperceptible atom in the infinite march to Thee. This is what Thy workers must never forget, otherwise they will become unfit to serve Thee. . . .

O my sweet Master, what childishness to think oneself responsible for anything at all and want to individualise Thy supreme and divine Will! Is it not enough to unite with Thy heart and live there permanently? Then Thou takest all the responsibilities and Thy will works without even our needing to know it. . . . Only a realisation independent of all outer circumstances, free from all attachment and all understanding, however high, is a true realisation, a valuable realisation. And the only such realisation is to unite with Thee integrally, closely, definitively. As for the care of Thy transitory, momentary manifestation in a fugitive existence and in a transient world, it is Thou who must be responsible for it and do what is necessary for it to exist, if Thou thinkest it good.

O my sweet Master, sovereign Lord, Thou hast taken away all my cares and left me only the Beatitude, the supreme ecstasy of Thy divine Communion.

July 18, 1914

TWO things remain unshakable despite all storm-winds, even the most violent: the will that all may be happy with the true happiness — Thine, and the ardent desire to unite perfectly and be identified with Thee. . . . All the rest is perhaps still the result of an effort and a pretension, this is spontaneous, unshakable; and just when it seems that the ground is giving way and everything breaking down, this appears luminous, pure and calm, piercing through the clouds, dispelling the shadows, emerging still greater and stronger from the ruins, carrying in itself Thy infinite Peace and Beatitude.

July 19, 1914

O LORD, Thou art the omnipotent Master of Thy own manifestation; grant to these instruments that they may escape from frames too narrow, from limits too fixed and mediocre. All the riches of human possibility are needed to translate even one atom of Thy infinite Force. . . . Open the doors that are closed, make the sealed fountains spring forth, that the floods of Thy eloquence and Thy beauty may overspread the world. Let there be amplitude and majesty, nobility and grace, charm and grandeur, variety and strength: for it is the will of the Lord to manifest.

O my sweet Master, Thou art the sovereign Ruler of our destinies; Thou art the omnipotent Master of Thy own manifestation.

Thine is all this world, Thine all these creatures and all these atoms. Transfigure them, illumine.

July 21, 1914

THERE was no longer any body, no longer any sensation; only a column of light was there, rising from where the base of the body normally is to where usually is the head, to form there a disk of light like that of the moon; then from there the column continued to rise very far above the head, opening out into an immense sun, dazzling and multicoloured, whence a rain of golden light fell covering all the earth.

Then slowly the column of light came down again forming an oval of living light, awakening and setting into movement — each one in a special way, according to a particular vibratory mode — the centres above the head, in the head, the throat, the heart, in the middle of the stomach, at the base of the spine and still farther down. At the level of the knees, the ascending and descending currents joined and the circulation thus went on uninterruptedly, enveloping the whole being in an immense oval of living light.

Then slowly the consciousness came down again, stage by stage, halting in each world, until the body-consciousness returned. The recovery of the body-consciousness was, if the memory is correct, the ninth stage. At that moment the body was still quite stiff and immobile.

July 22, 1914

THOU art all love, O Lord, and Thy love shines resplendently in the depths of every thought and every heart. Accomplish Thy work of transfiguration: illumine us. Open the still closed doors, widen the horizon, establish strength, unify our beings and make us participate in Thy divine beatitude that we may be able to make all men share in it. Grant that we may conquer the last obstacles, inner and outer, overcome the final difficulties. An ardent and sincere prayer has never risen in vain to Thee; always in Thy munificence Thou answerest every call and Thy mercy is infinite.

O divine Master, let Thy light fall into this chaos and bring forth from it a new world. Accomplish what is now in preparation and create a new humanity which may be the perfect expression of Thy new and sublime Law.

Nothing will stop our impetus; nothing will tire our effort; and, resting upon Thee all our hopes and all our activities, strong in our complete surrender to Thy Supreme Will, we shall march on to the conquest of Thy integral manifestation with the calm certitude of victory over all that would oppose it.

Hail to Thee, Master of the world, who triumphest over all darkness.

July 23, 1914

LORD, Thou art all-powerful: become the fighter, gain the victory. May Thy Love be the sovereign Master of our hearts and Thy Knowledge never leave our thoughts. . . . Do not abandon us to impotence and darkness; break every limit, shatter every chain, dispel every illusion.

Our aspiration rises to Thee in ardent prayer.

July 25, 1914

AT the rising of the sun I sang the praise of this world in which it is possible not only to desire Thee but to know Thee and even to become Thee. And I was astonished that there should be some who so ardently aspire to leave this universe and enter another world of perfection.

Thou hast placed such contentment in my heart that it has become impossible for me not to feel satisfied in all circumstances, inner or outer. And yet something in my being always aspires for more beauty, for more light, for more knowledge, for more love — in a word, for a more conscious, a more constant relation with Thee. . . . But this too depends upon Thy will, and when it is Thy will, Thou shalt grant me the entire transfiguration.

July 27, 1914

Humbly, quietly, my prayer rises to Thee, O sweet Master, Thou who acceptest without argument and without censure all that is offered to Thee, Thou who givest Thyself and makest Thyself known to all, without asking whether they are worthy of it or not, Thou who findest nothing too weak, too small, too modest, too inadequate to manifest Thee. . . .

Let me lay myself at Thy feet, let me melt into Thy heart and disappear in Thee, let me be annihilated in Thy beatitude, or rather let me be only Thy servant, claiming nothing more. I desire, I aspire for nothing else. To be only *Thy* servant is all I ask.

July 31, 1914

IT seems to me that Thou wouldst make me taste successively all the experiences which are ordinarily put at the summit of a Yoga as its culmination and the proof of its perfect accomplishment. The experience is striking, intense, complete; it carries within it the knowledge of all its effects, all its consequences; it is conscious, willed, the result of methodical effort and not of unexpected chance; and yet it is *always single of its kind*, like milestones set along a route which are separated from each other by a long ribbon of road; and, moreover, these milestones which mark the infinite ascent are never alike; they are always new and seem to have no connection one with the other. . . . Will a time come when Thou wilt make this being capable of synthetising all these countless experiences so as to draw from them a new realisation, more complete and more beautiful than all achieved so far? I do not know. But Thou hast taught me not to regret an exceptional state when it disappears any more than I desire it before it comes. I see in the disappearance no longer the sign of an instability in the progress made, but the evidence of a march which goes deliberately forward without stopping any longer than is indispensable for the various stages of the road.

Each time Thou teachest me yet a little better that the means of manifestation is limited only because we think it so, and that it can effectively partake of Thy infinitude; each time something of Thy immensity makes itself kin to the instrument which is its dwelling-place, flinging wide the doors which open on boundless horizons.

August 2, 1914

WHAT are these powerful gods whose hour of manifestation upon earth has come, if not the varied and perfected modes of Thy infinite activity, O Thou Master of all things, Being and Non-Being and What is beyond, Marvellous Unknowable One, our sovereign Lord? . . .

What are these manifold brilliant intellectual activities, these countless sunbeams illumining, conceiving and fashioning all forms, if not one of the modes of being of Thy infinite Will, one of the means of Thy manifestation, O Thou Master of our destinies, sole unthinkable Reality, sovereign Lord of all that is and all that is not yet. . . .

And all these mental powers, all these vital energies, and all these material elements, what are they if not Thyself in Thy outermost form, Thy ultimate modes of expression, of realisation, O Thou whom we adore devotedly and who escapest us on every side even while penetrating, animating and guiding us, Thou whom we cannot understand or define or name, Thou whom we cannot seize or embrace or conceive, and who art yet realised in our smallest acts. . . .

And all this enormous universe is only an atom of Thy eternal Will.

In the immensity of Thy effective Presence all things blossom!

August 3, 1914

ALL the being, this morning, is mute adoration and the immensity of Thy love fills its soul. . . .

The preparation and the work, the work and the preparation alternate and interpenetrate to such an extent that sometimes it becomes difficult to distinguish them; and their combination constitutes Thy divine life upon earth. What one must be, what one must do: the perfecting of Thy instrument and its utilisation go together; sometimes Thou wantest it to enrich itself and grow, to open all its doors on infinite horizons, to unite with the god it can manifest, to develop its power of conscious relation with the various worlds, and sometimes Thou wantest that, losing so to speak all consciousness of itself, it may be nothing but Thy force in action. And in the two is found the supreme law of communion with Thy will.

All the being, this morning, is mute adoration and the immensity of Thy love fills its soul.

215

August 4, 1914

O LORD, O eternal Master!

Men, driven by the conflict of forces, are performing a sublime sacrifice, they are offering their lives in a bloodstained holocaust. . . .

O Lord, O eternal Master, grant that all this may not be in vain, grant that the inexhaustible torrents of Thy divine Force may spread over the earth and penetrate its troubled atmosphere, the struggling energies, the violent chaos of battling elements; grant that the pure light of Thy Knowledge and the inexhaustible love of Thy Benediction may fill men's hearts, penetrate their souls, illumine their consciousness and, out of this obscurity, out of this sombre, terrible and potent darkness, bring forth the splendour of Thy majestic Presence!

My being is laid before Thee in a holocaust conscious and complete, that their unconscious holocaust may by it be made effective.

Accept the offering, answer our call: *Come*!

August 5, 1914

O ETERNAL Master, Thou art in all things like a vivifying breath, a sweet peace, a sun of luminous love piercing the clouds of darkness.

Grant that we may be Thy vivifying breath, Thy sweet peace, Thy luminous love upon the earth amidst our ignorant and sorrowful human brothers.

O divine Master, accept the offering of all myself as a holocaust that Thy work may be accomplished and the time may not pass by in vain.

In a serene ecstasy I give myself to Thee, that Thou mayst once again become the Master of what is Thine, the possessor of Thyself in each one of the countless atoms and in the consciousness that is synthetic and one.

O divine Master, accept this offering, this complete holocaust that the time may not have come in vain.

My whole being is transformed into a living flame, a flame of sacrifice of pure love.

Become once again the king of Thy kingdom, deliver the earth from the heavy weight which is crushing it, the weight of its own inert, ignorant, and obscure ill will.

O my sweet Master, my being is ablaze with the ardent flame of the sacrifice of love: accept my offering that the obstacle may be overcome.

August 6, 1914

WHAT then are the defects, the blemishes that prevent the offering from being complete enough for Thee to welcome it, the holocaust from seeming to Thee worthy to be received? . . . There are still some limitations in this being, but wilt Thou not shatter them?

O Lord, we know that it is an hour of great gravity for the earth: those who can be Thy intermediaries to it to make a greater harmony arise from the conflict and from its dark ugliness a diviner beauty, must be ready for the work. O Lord, O eternal Master, we entreat Thee, answer our endeavour, enlighten it, show us the way, give us the strength to break down all inner resistance and overcome every obstacle.

O my sweet Master, I prostrate myself at Thy feet; my entire being cries to Thee in an ardent supplication. . . . "Deliver me from the incapacity of the personal being."

August 8, 1914

MY pen is silent. . . . So absorbing is this material world! Why must we let it take so much place in our consciousness? Is it an incapacity in us? Is it Thy Will?

O my sweet Master, I would live only in Thee but Thou hast told me that I must live *for* Thee, and in thus living for Thee our consciousness turns towards external fields and we seem to go far from Thee.

I know this is not altogether true; but there is a resistance still in the being which refuses to yield, there is a door which remains closed, a certain door of luminous intelligence which no effort has been able till now to open, and this terribly impoverishes Thy manifestation.

When wilt Thou decide that the hour has come for all this resistance to disappear?

Monstrous forces have swooped down upon the earth like a hurricane, forces dark and violent and powerful and blind. Give us strength, O Lord, to illumine them. Thy splendour must break out everywhere in them and transfigure their action: their devastating passage must leave behind it a divine sowing. . . .

O my divine Master, do not reject my offering. Make me worthy to be wholly Thine in the plenitude of the giving and the fullness of the manifestation.

August 9, 1914

Lord, we are before Thee that Thy will may be done. Remove from our thought all obstacles, doubts, all weaknesses, limitations, all that veils our knowledge and obscures our understanding.

I am athirst for Thy consciousness, I am athirst for an integral union with Thee, not in inaction and a flight from physical activity but in a complete, absolute, perfect accomplishment of Thy will.

The splendour of Thy supreme light must spring forth from all the darkness that has swept down upon the earth.

August 11, 1914

O MY sweet Master, enter into all these confused
thoughts, all these anguished hearts; kindle there the fire
of Thy divine Presence. The shadow of the earth has fallen
back upon it, it has been completely shaken by it; but this
shadow was hiding Thy immutable sun, and now that it
has crashed down upon this poor world, rocking its very
foundations and transforming it into a formidable chaos,
wilt Thou not once again move upon the chaos and speak
Thy will: "Let there be Light"?

O Thou marvellous Unknown One, Thou who hast
not yet manifested Thyself, Thou who awaitest the propitious hour and hast sent us upon earth to prepare Thy
ways, all the elements of this being cry to Thee, "May Thy
will be done" and give themselves to Thee in a supreme,
unconquerable urge. . . .

Envelop this sorrowful earth with the strong arms of
Thy mercy, permeate it with the beneficent outpourings
of Thy infinite love.

I am the powerful arms of Thy mercy.

I am the vast bosom of Thy boundless love. . . . My
arms have enfolded the sorrowful earth and press it ten-
derly to my generous heart; and slowly a kiss of supreme
benediction is laid upon this struggling atom: the kiss of
the Mother which soothes and heals. . . .

August 13, 1914

THE being stands before Thee, with arms lifted, palms open, in an ardent aspiration.

O sweet Master, it is a Love more wonderful and formidable than any manifested so far which the earth needs; it is for this Love that it yearns. . . . Who will be capable and worthy of being its intermediary to it? Who? That matters little; but it must be done. O Lord, answer my call, accept the offering of my being despite its little worth and its limitations: Come.

More, always more; may the regenerating streams roll over the earth in beneficent waves. Transfigure and illumine. Work this supreme miracle so long awaited, and break all ignorant egoisms; awaken Thy sublime flame in every heart. Do not let us become benumbed in a tranquil serenity. We ought not to take any rest before Thy new and sovereign Love is manifested.

Listen to our prayer; answer our call: Come!

August 16, 1914

FOR three days I waited in an ardent prayer, hoping to see the new things . . . and all the obstacles surged up to veil, retard, deform Thy manifestation. And now we do not seem any nearer the goal than before.

O my sweet Master, why hast Thou told me to leave the blessed place in Thy heart and return to earth to attempt a realisation which everything seems to prove impossible? . . . What dost Thou expect of me that Thou hast torn me away from my divine and wonderful contemplation and plunged me again into this dark, struggling universe? When Thy force descends towards the earth in order to manifest, each one of the great Asuric beings who have resolved to be Thy servitors but preserved their nature's characteristic of domination and self-will, wants to pull it down for itself alone and distribute it to others afterwards; it always thinks it should be the sole or at least the supreme intermediary, and that the contact of all others with Thy Power cannot and should not be made except through its mediation. This unfortunate meanness is more or less conscious, but it is always there, delaying things indefinitely. If even for the greatest it is impossible in the integral manifestation to escape these lamentable limitations, why, O Lord, impose upon me the calvary of this constraint? . . . If Thou willest that it be thus, Thou shouldst rend the last veil and Thy splendour come in all its purity and transfigure the world!

Accomplish this miracle or else let me withdraw into Thee.

223

August 17, 1914

ALL errors, all prejudices, all misunderstandings must vanish in this whirlwind of destruction that is carrying away the past. . . . The light must become perfectly pure, free from all limitation, so that Thou canst manifest Thyself fully within it. Lord, Thou hast the Power and Thou wilt realise this supreme miracle. . . .

Into this consciousness Thou hast put the certitude of victory!

August 18, 1914

LET me turn to Thee in a profound and silent contemplation; let me place this integral being and its multiple activities at Thy feet as an offering; let me stop all the play of these forces, unify all these consciousnesses, so that one alone may persist, the one which is able to hear Thy command and understand it; let me plunge again into Thee as in a sovereignly beneficent sea, that which purifies from all ignorance. I feel as if I have gone down very deep into an unfathomable abyss of doubt and darkness, as if I am exiled from Thy eternal splendour; but I know that in this descent is the possibility of a higher ascent which will enable me to span a vaster horizon and draw a little nearer to Thy infinite heavens. Thy light is there, steady and guiding, shining without intermission in the depths of the abyss as in the luminous splendours; and a serene confidence, a calm indifference, a tranquil certitude dwell permanently in my consciousness. . . . I am like a boat which has long enjoyed the delights of the port and, despite the dark storm-laden clouds which hide the sun, unfurls its sails to launch forth into the great unknown, towards shores unheard of, towards new lands.

I am Thine, Lord, without any restriction or preference; may Thy will be done in all its rigorous plenitude; all my being adheres to it with a joyous acceptance and a calm serenity.

I have no longer any idea about the future: it is Thou who wilt awaken the new conception more closely answering Thy law.

In a most perfect surrender and a most entire trust I wait: Thy voice showing me Thy path.

August 20, 1914

To see the goal from a new angle which may usefully light up the others, we should constantly renew the experience of the inner discovery and return to the extreme limit of consciousness without at any time postulating beforehand what the end of our journey will be.

But instinctively the mind remembers the impression that it received from one or from some of the former contacts of our consciousness with the ultimate centre, and tells itself: "That is what one finds at the end of the road." It does not realise that the "That" which is in its thought is only one of countless ways of translating the goal or even of travestying it, nor does it perceive that the intellectual conception should follow the experience and not precede it.

To retrace the path in all innocence as though one had never before travelled it, is the true purity, the perfect sincerity — the sincerity that brings an uninterrupted progress, growth, an integral perfectioning.

Despite myself, in the silence of all thought, that is, of all conscious formulas, something in my being, deeper than words, turns to Thee, O ineffable Lord, in an ardent aspiration, giving Thee in offering all its activities, all its elements, all its modes of being, and imploring for all these the supreme illumination.

. . . O Thou, whom I cannot think, but whom with certitude I know!

August 21, 1914

O LORD, Lord, the whole earth is in an upheaval; it groans and suffers, it is in agony . . . all this suffering that has descended upon it must not be in vain; grant that all this bloodshed may produce a swifter germination of the seeds of beauty and light and love which must blossom and cover the earth with their rich harvest. Out of the depths of this abysm of darkness the whole being of the earth cries to Thee that Thou mayst give it air and light; it is stifling, wilt Thou not come to its aid?

O Lord, what must we do to triumph?

Hear us, for we must conquer at any price. Break down every resistance: appear!

August 24, 1914

LORD, it is in a heart-felt gratitude that I draw near to Thee. Thou hast given me the first words of the knowledge I so longed for, and with this knowledge has come effectivity, the true power in each field of realisation.

It is only a beginning, it is not an accomplishment; but the road opens, visible and straight, there is nothing to do but to follow it; the veil is rent in answer to the humble but all-powerful effort of the dark days. Grant, O Lord, that the path may be thus lit up for all, and that after having seen clearly into ourselves there may not be any new difficulties for the knowledge to become conscious in others. Despite everything, a human being, no matter how great, is limited, at least for a long time, by the very fact that he is human and because, even when he is in contact with immensity, this immensity is translated in his outer consciousness from the angle of his own personality. It is very difficult for him not to have a perspective partially obliterated as it were by his own viewpoint. But these last obstacles must be overcome, definitively broken down, so that they may no longer be able to rise again. The road must be entirely free and the knowledge that has been glimpsed become firmly established. Thy grace is with us, Lord, and it never leaves us, even when appearances are dark; night is sometimes necessary to prepare more perfect dawns. But perhaps this time Thou hast placed us in the presence of the Dawn that does not pass away. . . .

Receive the offerings of our ardent gratitude and our integral surrender.

I knew that this notebook would end with the closing of one phase of my spiritual life. That is indeed what is happening.

The light has come, the road has opened; with a grateful bow to the laborious past, we shall move swiftly forward on the new way opened wide by Thee before us.

On the threshold of this new field of a vaster and more conscious realisation, we bow before Thee, O Lord, in an integral surrender and adoration. We give ourselves to Thee without reservation.

Once again it is Thou who livest in us, and Thou alone. Thou hast once more become the King of Thy kingdom, but a kingdom vaster and more perfect, a kingdom more worthy of Thy rule.

August 25, 1914

O LORD, let Thy Will be done, Thy work be accomplished. Fortify our devotion, increase our surrender, give us light upon the path. We erect Thee within us as our supreme Master that Thou mayst become supreme Master of all the earth.

Our speech is still ignorant: enlighten it.

Our aspiration is still imperfect: purify it.

Our action is still powerless: make it effective.

O Lord, the earth groans and suffers; chaos has made this world its abode.

The darkness is so deep that Thou alone canst dispel it. Come, manifest Thyself, that Thy work may be accomplished.

August 26, 1914

O MY sweet Master, O Lord of Felicity, all these worlds of felicity interpenetrating and completing one another are an immensity difficult to perceive in their totality. Give us the knowledge of these laws, give us the power to awaken the earth to an understanding and perception of the aim so blindly pursued.

In all things Thou art the happiness without alloy, a blessed felicity . . . but the felicity is perfect only when it is integral, from the most external manifestations down into the most unfathomable depths.

O Lord, Thou hast placed me on a threshold of wonder; confirm me in this knowledge. Establish me in that centre of consciousness whence all my activities will be an unmixed expression of Thy law.

In a potent and mute adoration, I wait.

August 27, 1914*

To be the divine love, love powerful, infinite, unfathomable, in every activity, in all the worlds of being — it is for this I cry to Thee, O Lord. Let me be consumed with this love divine, love powerful, infinite, unfathomable, in every activity, in all the worlds of being! Transmute me into that burning brazier so that all the atmosphere of earth may be purified with its flame.

Oh, to be Thy Love infinitely. . . .

August 28, 1914

O LORD, O eternal Master, my thought lies mute and powerless before Thee but my heart calls to Thee; awaken all my being that it may be for Thee, entirely, the needed instrument, the perfect servitor.

Oh, to be infinitely Thou, Thou in all things, Thou everywhere, Thou always, the absolute silence, the absolute movement . . .

To be nothing other than the One, all-containing, contained in all — free from every limitation and from all blindness.

O Supreme Triumphant, triumph over every obstacle.

August 29, 1914

WHAT would be the use of man if he were not created to throw a bridge between That which *is* eternally but is unmanifested and that which is manifested, between all the transcendences and splendours of the divine life and all the dark and sorrowful ignorance of the material world? Man is the link between What must be and what is; he is the footbridge thrown across the abyss, he is the great cross-shaped X, the quaternary connecting link. His true domicile, the effective seat of his consciousness should be in the intermediary world at the meeting-point of the four arms of the cross, just where all the infinitude of the Unthinkable comes to take a precise form so that it may be projected into the innumerable manifestation. . . .

That centre is a place of supreme love, of perfect consciousness, of pure and total knowledge. There establish, O Lord, those who can, who must and truly want to serve Thee, so that Thy work may be accomplished, the bridge definitively established, and Thy forces poured unwearyingly over the world.

August 31, 1914*

IN this formidable disorder and terrible destruction can be seen a great working, a necessary toil preparing the earth for a new sowing which will rise in marvellous spikes of grain and give to the world the shining harvest of a new race. . . . The vision is clear and precise, the plan of Thy divine law so plainly traced that peace has come back and installed itself in the hearts of the workers. There are no more doubts and hesitations, no longer any anguish or impatience. There is only the grand straight line of the work eternally accomplishing itself in spite of all, against all, despite all contrary appearances and illusory detours. These physical personalities, moments unseizable in the infinite Becoming, know that they will have made humanity take one farther step, infallibly and without care for the inevitable results, whatever be the apparent momentary consequences: they unite themselves with Thee, O Master eternal, they unite themselves with Thee, O Mother universal, and in this double identity with That which is beyond and That which is all the manifestation they taste the infinite joy of the perfect certitude.

Peace, peace in all the world. . . .
War is an appearance,
Turmoil is an illusion,
Peace is there, immutable peace.

Mother, sweet Mother who I am, Thou art at once the destroyer and the builder.

The whole universe lives in Thy breast with all its life innumerable and Thou livest in Thy immensity in the least of its atoms.

And the aspiration of Thy infinitude turns towards That which is not manifested to cry to it for a manifestation ever more complete and more perfect.

All *is*, in one time, in a triple and clairvoyant total Consciousness, the Individual, the Universal, the Infinite.

September 1, 1914*

O MOTHER Divine, with what fervour, what ardent love I came to Thee in Thy deepest consciousness, in Thy high status of sublime love and perfect felicity, and I nestled so close into Thy arms and loved Thee with so intense a love that I became altogether Thyself. Then in the silence of our mute ecstasy a voice from yet profounder depths arose and the voice said, "Turn towards those who have need of thy love." All the grades of consciousness appeared, all the successive worlds. Some were splendid and luminous, well ordered and clear; there knowledge was resplendent, expression was harmonious and vast, will was potent and invincible. Then the worlds darkened in a multiplicity more and more chaotic, the Energy became violent and the material world obscure and sorrowful. And when in our infinite love we perceived in its entirety the hideous suffering of the world of misery and ignorance, when we saw our children locked in a sombre struggle, flung upon each other by energies that had deviated from their true aim, we willed ardently that the light of Divine Love should be made manifest, a transfiguring force at the centre of these distracted elements. Then, that the will might be yet more powerful and effective, we turned towards Thee, O unthinkable Supreme, and we implored Thy aid. And from the unsounded depths of the Unknown a reply came sublime and formidable and we knew that the earth *was saved*.

September 4, 1914

DARKNESS has descended upon the earth, thick, violent, victorious . . . All is sadness, terror, destruction in the physical world, and the splendour of Thy light of love seems darkened by a veil of mourning. . . .

O sweet Mother, I merge into Thee in an immense love and an intense supplication to the Lord of all things that HE may show us the way, that HE may trace out for us the path of His work, so that we may tread it boldly.

Time presses: the divine powers must come, O Lord, to the help of the agonised earth.

O Mother, sweet Mother, Thou dost clasp all Thy children close to Thy vast breast, and Thy love enfolds them all alike.

I have become the purifying fire of Thy love. O Lord, silent Unthinkable One, accept the holocaust of this brazier of love, that Thy reign may come, Thy light triumph over darkness and death.

Manifest Thy power. From day to day, from hour to hour we implore Thee: "O Lord, manifest Thy power!"

September 5, 1914

"FACE the danger!" Thou saidst to me, "why dost thou wish to turn away thy gaze or flee far away from action, flee from the battle, into the deep contemplation of Truth? It is its integral manifestation which must be realised, its victory over all the obstacles of blind ignorance and dark hostility. Look the danger straight in the face and it will vanish before the Power."

O Lord, I understood the weakness of this most external nature which is always ready to surrender material things and escape, as a compensation, into a supreme intellectual and spiritual independence. But Thou expectest action from us, and action does not allow such an attitude. It is not enough to triumph in the inner worlds, we must triumph right down to the most material worlds. We must not flee from the difficulty or obstacle, because we have the power to do so by taking refuge in the consciousness where there are no obstacles. . . . We must look the danger straight in the face with faith in Thy Omnipotence, and Thy Omnipotence will triumph.

Give me integrally the heart of the fighter, O Lord, and Thy victory is sure.

"Conquer at any price" should be the present motto. Not because one is attached to the work and its results, not because one needs such an action, not because one is incapable of escaping from all contingencies.

240

But because Thou hast commanded action from us. But because the hour of Thy triumph upon earth has come. But because Thou willest the integral victory. And in an infinite love for the world . . . let us fight!

September 6, 1914

HIGHER, ever higher! Let us never be satisfied with what is achieved, let us not stop at any realisation, let us march always onwards, ceaselessly, energetically, towards an ever completer manifestation, an ever higher and more total consciousness. . . . Yesterday's victory must be only a stepping-stone to the victory of tomorrow, and the power of the day gone by a weakness beside the effectivity to come.

O Mother Divine, Thy march is triumphal and uninterrupted. He who unites with Thee in integral love journeys unceasingly towards ever vaster horizons, towards an ever completer realisation, leaping from peak to peak in the splendour of Thy light, to the conquest of the marvellous secrets of the Unknown and their integral manifestation.

O divine Victor, all the earth sings Thy praises, and all forces will obey Thee.

For the Lord has said: "The hour has come."

And all obstacles will be surmounted.

September 9, 1914

THE world is divided between two opposite forces struggling for supremacy, and both are equally against Thy law, O Lord; for Thou dost not want either mortal stagnation or blind destruction. It is in a constant, progressive and luminous transformation that Thou expressest Thyself; and it is this we must establish upon earth if we want to manifest Thy will.

At times our impatience would like to know immediately the means of this manifestation. But our impatience is futile and receives no answer. For the knowledge will come at the opportune moment, at the moment of action.

Hence it is with the thought at peace and with the realising will calm and strong that we await the sign Thou wilt give us.

September 10, 1914

THY love is like a rising tide, invading the entire being and breaking upon all things. Lord, Thy love will penetrate all hearts and kindle in them the divine flame which never goes out, the divine beauty which does not fade, and, above every contrast and contradiction, it will establish in all that unchanging Bliss which is the supreme good.

Thy light is like a rising tide, invading the entire being and breaking upon all things. Lord, Thy light will penetrate all thoughts and create in them that sovereign clarity which does not waver, the divine clear-sightedness which never errs, and, above every contrast and contradiction, it will establish in all the splendour of Thy knowledge which is the supreme wisdom.

Thy force is like a rising tide, invading the entire being and breaking upon all things. Lord, Thy force will penetrate all life and create in it the effective strength which never fails, the divine power which is invincible, and, above every contrast and contradiction, it will establish in all Thy mastering energy which is the supreme will.

September 13, 1914

WITH fervour I hail Thee, O divine Mother, and in deep affection identify myself with Thee. United with our divine Mother I turn, O Lord, to Thee, and bow to Thee in mute adoration and in an ardent aspiration identify myself with Thee.

Then all becomes a marvellous Silence; Being is absorbed in Non-Being, all is suspended, at rest, motionless. How shall one express the inexpressible?

September 14, 1914

THERE is no longer an "I", no longer an individuality, no longer any personal limits. There is only the immense universe, our sublime Mother, burning with an ardent fire of purification in honour of Thee, O Lord, divine Master, sovereign Will, so that this Will may meet with no farther obstacle in the way of its realisation.

A mighty canticle of fervent love and exultation arises to Thee, O Lord, all the earth in an inexpressible ecstasy unites with Thee.

Let Thy potent breath feed the brazier, that it may become ever vaster and more formidable, that all darkness and blind resistance may be absorbed, set ablaze, transfigured into Light in the marvellous purifying flame.

Oh, the peace-giving splendour of Thy purification!

September 16, 1914

HEARKEN to the voice that rises, hearken to the chant that is lifted up to hail Thy divine Dawn.

Let the supreme Law be fulfilled; whether it be existence eternal, universal, or re-absorption into Non-Being matters little. Must one choose between the two? I cannot; in my consciousness there is no longer any preference, only one Will persists — Thine, O Ineffable.

And all this universe is now only a chant, ever vaster and more harmonious, arising to salute Thy divine Dawn.

247

September 17, 1914

No longer can any impulse to action come from outside or from any particular world. It is Thou, Lord, who settest all things in motion from the depths of the being, it is Thy will which directs, Thy force which acts; and no longer in the limited field of a small individual consciousness but in the universal field of a consciousness which, in every state of being, is united with the whole. And the being has at once the conscious perception of all universal movements in their complexity and even their confusion, and the silent and perfect peace of Thy sovereign immutability.

September 20, 1914

MY pen is mute, for thought is silent, but my heart aspires to Thee, O Lord, uniting Thee with our divine Mother in one love, one veneration. And through Thee the entire being strains towards the Ineffable; beyond Being, beyond the very Silence, that is united with That.

September 22, 1914

O LORD, Thou who art on the threshold of the Un-knowable, I greet Thee!

And is it not Thou greeting Thy own self in the Un-thinkable Essence of Being, in its immeasurable depths, and even in its most external realisations? For the Be-ing is Thyself, whatever its mode of existence, and the Unthinkable Eternal is also Thyself in Thy essence. And this integral consciousness Thou hast made ours, so that we may be Thyself, not only in fact but consciously and effectively. And thus all is an interchange of salutations full of love and joyous adoration, in an ardent aspiration of our Mother towards Thee and an infinite and power-ful response from Thee to our Mother, and finally from the totality of Thyself to all that is not yet manifested, to all the Unknowable which we shall know more and more, better and better, but which will ever remain the Unknowable.

In the absolute silence all is, now and eternally; in the universal manifestation all will be in a perpetual becoming.

In the perfection of consciousness and the integral life, the being sings a canticle of gladness for That which at once is and will be eternally.

Hail to Thee, Master of the world, art Thou not the in-termediary between what is and what will be, even while being simultaneously what is and what will be?

O marvellous Immensity, perceptible and indefinable at once, in an integral illumination I bow to Thee.

September 24, 1914

HOW present Thou art in our midst, beloved Mother! It is as if Thou wouldst assure us of Thy complete assistance, as if Thou wouldst show us that the Will which means to manifest through us, has found in us instruments which can realise Its Law, by placing it in complete accordance with Thy present possibilities. The things which seemed most difficult, most improbable, perhaps even most impossible, become wholly realisable, because Thy Presence is our assurance that the material world itself is prepared to manifest the new form of the Will and the Law.

I greet Thee in the joyful plenitude of perfect harmony — Thee, Thy Principle and Thy works.

September 25, 1914*

O DIVINE and adorable Mother, with Thy help what is there that is impossible? The hour of realisations is near and Thou hast assured us of Thy aid that we may perform integrally the supreme Will.

Thou hast accepted us as fit intermediaries between the unthinkable realities and the relativities of the physical world, and Thy constant presence in our midst is a token of Thy active collaboration.

The Lord has willed and Thou dost execute:

A new Light shall break upon the earth.

A new world shall be born,

And the things that were promised shall be fulfilled.

September 28, 1914*

MY pen is mute to chant Thy presence, O Lord; yet art Thou like a king who has taken entire possession of his kingdom. Thou art there, organising, putting all in place, developing and increasing every province. Thou awakenest those that were asleep. Thou makest active those that were sinking towards inertia; Thou art building a harmony out of the whole. A day will come when the harmony shall be achieved and all the country shall be by its very life the bearer of Thy word and Thy manifestation.

But meanwhile my pen is mute to chant Thy praise.

September 30, 1914

LORD, Thou hast broken down the barriers of thought and the realisation has appeared in all its amplitude. Not to forget any of its aspects, to carry out their accomplishment at the same time, without neglecting any of them, not to allow any limitation, any restriction to come in the way and delay our march, this is what Thou wilt help us to do through Thy supreme intervention. And all those who are Thyself, manifesting Thee in the perfection of some particular activity, will also be our collaborators, for such is Thy Will.

Our Divine Mother is with us and has promised us identification with the supreme and total consciousness — from the unfathomable depths to the most external world of the senses. And in all these domains Agni assures us of the help of his purifying flame, destroying all obstacles, kindling the energies, stimulating the will, so that the realisation may be hastened. Indra is with us for the perfection of the illumination in our knowledge; and the divine Soma has transformed us in his infinite, sovereign, marvellous love, bringer of the supreme beatitudes. . . .

O divine and sweet Mother, I bow to Thee with a rapt, ineffable tenderness, and with infinite trust.

O splendid Agni, Thou who art so living within me, I call Thee, I invoke Thee that Thou mayst be more living still, that Thy brazier may become more immense, Thy flames higher and more powerful, that the entire being may now be only an ardent burning, a purifying pyre.

O Indra, I venerate and admire Thee, I implore Thee

254

that Thou mayst unite with me, that Thou mayst definitively break down all the barriers of thought, that Thou mayst bestow upon me the divine knowledge.

*O Thou, Sublime Love, to whom I gave never any other name, but who art so wholly the very substance of my being, Thou whom I feel vibrant and alive in the least of my atoms even as in the infinite universe and beyond, Thou who breathest in every breath, movest in the heart of all activities, art radiant through all that is of good will and hidden behind all sufferings, Thou for whom I cherish a cult without limit which grows ever more intense, permit that I may with more and more reason feel that I am Thyself wholly.

And Thou, O Lord, who art all this made one and much more, O sovereign Master, extreme limit of our thought, who standest for us at the threshold of the Unknown, make rise from that Unthinkable some new splendour, some possibility of a loftier and more integral realisation, that Thy work may be accomplished and the universe take one step farther towards the sublime Identity, the supreme Manifestation.

And now my pen falls mute and I adore Thee in silence.*

October 5, 1914 *

IN the calm silence of Thy contemplation, O Divine Master, Nature is fortified and tempered anew. All principle of individuality is overpassed, she is plunged in Thy infinity that allows oneness to be realised in all domains without confusion, without disorder. The combined harmony of that which persists, that which progresses and that which eternally is, is little by little accomplished in an always more complex, more extended and more lofty equilibrium. And this interchange of the three modes of life allows the plenitude of the manifestation.

Many seek Thee at this hour in anguish and incertitude. May I be their mediator with Thee that Thy light may illumine them, that Thy peace may appease. My being is now only a point of support for Thy action and a centre for Thy consciousness. Where now are the limits, whither have fled the obstacles? Thou art the sovereign Lord of Thy kingdom.

October 6, 1914

O SWEET Mother, Thou shouldst teach me to be integrally and constantly Thyself, entirely consecrated to the giving of an ever more perfect means of expression to That which wills to manifest. . . .

All is calm, serene; there is no more struggle, no more anguish; aspiration itself becomes sovereignly peaceful in its immensity, yet loses nothing of its intensity; and through a curious opposition in the consciousness, like the obverse and reverse sides of a medal, the being perceives at one and the same time, the immutable calm of the infinite Reality in which all is for ever without any possibility of change, and the ardent and rapid march of all that becomes without cessation in an uninterrupted progression . . . And to Thee, O Lord, both are equally true.

October 7, 1914 *

OH, let Light be poured on all the earth and Peace inhabit every heart. . . . Almost all know only the material life heavy, inert, conservative, obscure; their vital forces are so tied to this physical form of existence that, even when left to themselves and outside the body, they are still solely occupied with these material contingencies that are yet so harassing and painful. . . . Those in whom the mental life is awakened are restless, tormented, agitated, arbitrary, despotic. Caught altogether in the whirl of the renewals and transformations of which they dream, they are ready to destroy everything without knowledge of any foundation on which to construct, and with their light made only of blinding flashes they increase yet more the confusion rather than help it to cease.

In all there lacks the unchanging peace of Thy sovereign contemplation and the calm vision of Thy immutable eternity.

And with the infinite gratitude of the individual being to whom Thou hast accorded this surpassing grace, I implore Thee, O Lord, that under cover of the present turmoil, in the very heart of this extreme confusion the miracle may be accomplished and Thy law of supreme serenity and pure unchanging light become visible to the perception of all and govern the earth in a humanity at last awakened to Thy divine consciousness.

O sweet Master, Thou hast heard my prayer, Thou wilt reply to my call.

October 8, 1914

THE joy that is contained in activity is compensated and balanced by the perhaps still greater joy contained in withdrawal from all activity; when the two states alternate in the being or are even simultaneously conscious, the felicity is complete, for then, O Lord, Thy plenitude is realised.

O divine Master, Thou hast granted to me the infinitude of divine contemplation, the perfect calm of Thy Eternity, and through an identification with our divine Mother, the All-Realiser, Thou hast permitted me to participate in her sovereign power to be conscious and active ...

In the omnipotent bliss of Thy infinitude, I bow to Thee!

October 10, 1914

MAY the offering of my being, constantly renewed and growing more and more integral, be laid before the Supreme Reality, the Unthinkable who cannot be formulated, but who, in time, expresses himself eternally in an ever completer and more perfect manifestation. O Thou whom I cannot name, Thou whose will I perceive in supreme silence and total surrender, let me be the representative of all the earth, so that, united with my consciousness, it may give itself unreservedly to Thee.

Thou art the perfect peace and the marvellous accomplishment; Thou art all that the universe is, immutably, beyond time, and wants to be more and more in the consciousness of time and space. Thou art all that is in the infinite stillness and the divine hope of all that wants to be. . . . Lord, dispense to the world Thy unbelievable boons.

Peace, peace upon all the earth!

October 11, 1914

WHY this persistent feeling so tinged with uneasiness and expectancy? The being, entirely turned to Thee, lives in the beatitude of the divine communion; all is calm, serene, strong, sovereignly peaceful; all is light in widened horizons and, in silent contemplation, my devotion has become intenser yet. What then is this sensation which seems as though grafted upon the being and takes on the appearance of a warning given to a consciousness insufficiently awakened in the domain of Matter?

I ask why, O Lord, and yet I know that if it is necessary for me to understand the reason, Thou hast already told it to me and only my incapacity keeps me from knowing it; or else to know it is neither useful nor even helpful for me, and in this case nothing will reply to my question. . . .

But the peace becomes more sovereign still and in an infinite harmony the being takes on its supreme amplitude.

O Lord, with what fervour I greet Thee!

October 12, 1914

IT was their sorrow and suffering which the physical
being was feeling, Lord. When will ignorance dissolve?
When will pain cease? O Lord, grant that each element
of the universe may become conscious of its principle
of being and, without disappearing, be transformed; may
the veils of egoistic blindness which hide Thee be removed
and mayst Thou appear resplendent in the total manifestation. All this is eternally in Thy absolute silence; but it
is through an infinite progression that it manifests in the
integral consciousness.

October 14, 1914*

MOTHER Divine, Thou art with us; every day Thou givest me the assurance and, closely united in an identity that grows more and more total, more and more constant, we turn to the Lord of the Universe and to That which is beyond in a great aspiration towards the new Light. All the earth is in our arms like a sick child who must be cured and for whom one has a special affection because of his very weakness. Cradled on the immensity of the eternal becomings, ourselves those becomings, we contemplate hushed and glad the eternity of the immobile Silence where all is realised in the perfect Consciousness and immutable Existence, miraculous gate of all the unknown that is beyond.

Then is the veil torn, the inexpressible Glory uncovered and, suffused with the ineffable Splendour, we turn back towards the world to bring it the glad tidings.

Lord, Thou hast given me the happiness infinite. What being, what circumstance can have the power to take it away from me?

October 16, 1914

IT is Thy Will that I should be like a channel, always
open, always wider, through which Thy forces may pour
themselves in abundance on the world. . . . O Lord, let
Thy Will be done. Am I not Thy Will and Thy Consciousness in a felicity supreme? . . .

The being grows immeasurably in largeness and becomes vast like the universe.

October 17, 1914

O MOTHER divine, the obstacles shall be overcome, the enemies appeased; Thou shalt dominate the whole earth with Thy sovereign love, and every consciousness shall be illumined with Thy serenity.

This is the promise.

October 23, 1914

O LORD, the entire being is ready and it calls Thee to take possession of what is Thine; of what service can be the instrument if the Master will not use it? And whatever be the mode of manifestation, it shall be well, from the most humble, most obscure, most material, most outwardly limited, to the vastest, most brilliant, most powerful, most intellectual.

The entire being is ready and waits in a passive silence until it is Thy Will to manifest.

October 25, 1914*

MY aspiration to Thee, O Lord, has taken the form of a beautiful rose, harmonious, full in bloom, rich in fragrance. I stretch it out to Thee with both arms in a gesture of offering and I ask of Thee: If my understanding is limited, widen it; if my knowledge is obscure, enlighten it; if my heart is empty of ardour, set it aflame; if my love is insignificant, make it intense; if my feelings are ignorant and egoistic, give them the full consciousness in the Truth. And the "I" which demands this of Thee, O Lord, is not a little personality lost amidst thousands of others. It is the whole earth that aspires to Thee in a movement full of fervour.

In the perfect silence of my contemplation all widens to infinity, and in the perfect peace of that silence Thou appearest in the resplendent glory of Thy Light.

November 3, 1914

FOR quite a long time, Lord, my pen had fallen silent. . . . Yet hast Thou given me hours of unforgettable illumination, hours in which the union between the most divine Consciousness and the most material grew perfect, hours when the identification of the individual being with the universal Mother and of the universal Mother with Thee was so complete that the individual consciousness could perceive simultaneously its own existence, the life of the entire universe and Thy eternity beyond all change. Beatitude was at its height in an ineffable and infinite peace, the consciousness luminous and immeasurable, complex and yet one, existence all-powerful, master of death. And this is no longer a fleeting state, attained after a long concentration, vanishing as soon as it is born; it is a state that can last long hours full of eternity, hours at once instantaneous and interminable, a state brought about at will, that is to say, one which is permanent, one with which the most external consciousness comes into contact as soon as any occasion allows it, as soon as it is no longer occupied with a definite intellectual or physical task. In all work, constantly, there is the perception of Thy invariable presence in Thy dual form of Non-Being and Being, but as though behind a fine veil woven by the indispensable concentration upon the work that is done; while in the hours of solitude the being is immediately enveloped by a marvellously powerful atmosphere, limpid, calm, divine; it lies merged within it, and then the life of splendour begins again in all its amplitude, all its complexity, all its sublimity; the physical body is glorified, supple, vigorous, energetic; the mind is superbly active in its calm lucidity, guiding and transmitting the forces of Thy divine Will; and all the being exults in an endless beatitude, a boundless love, a sovereign power, a perfect knowledge, an infinite consciousness. . . . It is Thyself and Thou alone who livest, even in the least atom of the body-substance itself.

Thus the solid foundations of Thy terrestrial work are prepared, the substructure of the immense edifice built; in every corner of the world one of Thy divine stones is laid by the power of conscious and formative thought; and in the hour of realisations the earth, thus prepared, will be ready to receive the sublime temple of Thy new and more complete manifestation.

November 8, 1914*

FOR the plenitude of Thy Light we invoke Thee, O Lord! Awaken in us the power to express Thee.

All is mute in the being as in a desert crypt; but in the heart of the shadow, in the bosom of the silence burns the lamp that can never be extinguished, the fire of an ardent aspiration to know Thee and totally to live Thee.

The nights follow the days, new dawns unweariedly succeed to past dawns, but always there mounts the scented flame that no storm-wind can force to vacillate. Higher it climbs and higher and one day attains the vault still closed, the last obstacle opposing our union. And so pure, so erect, so proud is the flame that suddenly the obstacle is dissolved.

Then Thou appearest in all Thy splendour, in the dazzling force of Thy infinite glory; at Thy contact the flame changes into a column of light that chases the shadows away for ever.

And the Word leaps forth, a supreme revelation.

November 9, 1914

O LORD, for perfect consciousness we aspire . . .
  All the being is gathered into a well-tied sheaf made of various but harmonised flowers. The will was the hand that gathered the flowers and the tie that bound the sheaf and it is the will that now holds it out to Thee like a scented offering. To Thee it is held out unweariedly, without faltering.

November 10, 1914

O LORD, Thy Presence is settled within me like an unshakable rock; and the whole being exults in belonging to Thee without the least reserve, with a wide and complete surrender.

O Consciousness, immobile and serene, Thou watchest at the confines of the world like the sphinx of eternity. And yet to some Thou yieldest Thy secret.

They can become Thy sovereign Will which chooses without preference, executes without desire.

November 15, 1914

THE one important thing is the goal to be reached; the road matters little, and often it is preferable not to know it beforehand. But what we need to know is whether the time for the divine action upon earth has really come, and whether the work conceived in the depths can be realised.

Of this, O Lord, Thou hast given us the assurance, an assurance which has been accompanied by the most powerful promise that Nature, the universal Consciousness can possibly make. . . . Thus we have the certitude that what must be done will be done and that our present individual beings are in reality called upon to collaborate in this glorious victory, this new manifestation. What more do we need to know? Nothing. So it is with the greatest confidence that we can witness the formidable fight, the onslaught of the adverse forces, which, unknowingly, finally serve in the realisation of Thy plan. We would be wrong to feel anxious because it is not given to us to know how it serves Thy plan and by what means Thou wilt triumph over all resistances; for Thy triumph is so perfect that every obstacle, every ill-will, every hatred raised up against Thee is a promise of a still vaster and more complete victory.

From the sum of resistances, one can gauge the scope Thou wouldst give to the action of that among Thy pure forces which is coming to manifest upon earth. What opposes is just that upon which it is the mission of these forces to act; it is the darkest hatred which must be touched and transformed into luminous peace.

If the human individual Thou hast chosen as Thy centre of action and Thy intermediary meets with few obstacles, few misunderstandings and little hatred, it means that Thou hast entrusted to him a limited mission without any intensity. It is in the narrow circle of already prepared men of goodwill that he will act and not upon the chaotic and confused mass of terrestrial substance.

O divine Master, this knowledge which Thou hast given me, let all of us share, so that the peace of conviction may reign in our hearts and we may, in the calm of Thy sovereign certitude, confront with head held high all that, unconsciously attracted to the transfiguration, plunges headlong into blind ignorance, believing it will be able to destroy the Transfiguring Love.

November 16, 1914

THOU art like the wind upon the sea, driving the boat back ashore until it is at last loaded with all the goods necessary for the long voyage. Thou wouldst not have us embark thoughtlessly. Thy servitors must be ready for all eventualities, must be capable of answering all demands, satisfying all needs.

November 17, 1914

ALAS, sublime Mother, how great must be Thy patience! Each time Thy conscious will attempts to manifest itself in order to rectify errors, to hasten the uncertain progress of the individual led astray by his own illusion of knowledge, to trace the sure path and give him the strength to walk steadily upon it without stumbling, almost always he pushes Thee away as a tiresome and short-sighted adviser. He is willing to love Thee in theory with a vague and inconsistent love, but his proud mind refuses to confide in Thee and prefers to wander all by itself rather than advance guided by Thee.

And Thou repliest, ever smiling in Thy unwearying benevolence: "This intellectual faculty which makes man proud and leads him into error is the very same which, once enlightened and purified, can also lead him farther, higher than universal nature, to a direct and conscious communion with our Lord, with That which is beyond all manifestation. This dividing intellect, which makes him stand apart from me, also enables him to scale rapidly the heights he must climb, without letting his progress be enchained and delayed by the totality of the universe, which, in its immensity and complexity, cannot effect so swift an ascent."

O Divine Mother, always Thy word comforts and blesses, calms and illumines, and Thy generous hand lifts a fold of the veil hiding the infinite knowledge.

How calm, noble and pure is the splendour of Thy perfect contemplation!

November 20, 1914

O H, I would be before Thee, Lord, always like an absolutely blank page, so that Thy will may be written in me without any difficulty, any mixture.

The very remembrance of past experiences should sometimes be swept away from the thought so as not to obstruct this work of perpetual reconstruction which alone in a world of relativities permits Thy perfect manifestation.

Often one clings to that which was, fearing to lose the result of a precious experience, to give up a vast and high consciousness, to fall back into a lower state.

And yet, what should he fear who is Thine? Can he not walk with joyful soul and illumined brow upon the path Thou tracest for him, whatever it may be, even if this path be altogether incomprehensible to his limited reason?

O Lord, break the old frames of thought, abolish past experiences, dissolve the conscious synthesis if Thou thinkest it necessary, so that Thy work may be accomplished better and better, Thy service upon earth be perfected.

November 21, 1914

O LORD, Thou hast given me Thy Power that Thy Peace and Joy may reign over the world.

And this being is now only an embrace of peace enveloping the whole earth, an ocean of joy breaking over all things.

O you who are full of hatred, rancour shall be effaced from your hearts as the sea effaces an imprint upon the sands.

O you who feed upon vengeance, peace shall pass into your hearts as it enters the soul of a child rocked by its mother.

For the divine and universal Mother has turned her gaze upon the earth and she has blessed it.

December 4, 1914

AFTER long days of silence, entirely occupied by outer work, it is at last given to me to resume these pages and continue with Thee, Lord, this conversation which is so sweet to me. . . .

But Thou hast broken all my habits, for Thou wouldst prepare me for liberation from every mental form. Certain mental forms, more particularly powerful or adapted to the temperament, are sure guides to supreme experiences. But once the experiences are over, Thou wouldst have them free in themselves from bondage to any mental form, however high or pure it may be, so as to be capable of expression in the new, most true form, that is, the one most suitable to the experience.

So Thou didst break all my forms of thought, and I found myself before Thee stripped of all mental constructions, as ignorant about this as a new-born child; and in the darkness of this void lay once again the sovereign peace of something which is not expressed in words but which IS. And I wait without impatience and without fear, for Thee to construct once again from the heart of the unfathomable depths the intellectual form which seems to Thee the most suitable for manifesting Thee in this instrument moulded out of surrender and ardent faith.

And before this immense night full of promise, I feel, more than I have ever felt before, free and vast, infinitely. . . .

And in a supreme beatitude I offer Thee thanks, O Lord, for the marvellous favour Thou hast bestowed upon me: that of being before Thee like a new-born child.

December 10, 1914

LISTEN, O Lord . . . in the silence of deep meditation
my prayer rises ardently to Thee.

Is it not a great folly to become identified with one
form of thought, one mental construction, however vast
and powerful it may be, to the point of making it the
living centre of one's being, one's experience and activity? Truth is eternally beyond all that we can think or
say of it. To endeavour to find the most suitable expression, the one best adapted to this truth, is of course a
useful task, even an indispensable one for the integrality of one's own development and that of all humanity;
but one must always feel free in front of this expression,
have one's centre of consciousness above it, in the reality
which, despite the grandeur, the beauty, the perfection
of a mental formula, always eludes every formula. The
world is not what we think it to be. The importance
of the idea we have of it lies in its effect on our attitude towards action; and this attitude may come from
a much deeper, truer, more unchanging inspiration than
that resulting from a mental construction, however powerful it may be. To feel in oneself the will to express
for men the eternal Truth in a completer, higher, more
exact form than all those which have preceded it, is
good; but on condition that one does not identify one's
"self" with this work to the point of being its slave
and losing before it all independence and self-control.
It is just an activity and nothing more, whatever may
be its importance from the earthly point of view; but

281

it must not be forgotten that it is relative like all activities and that we should not allow it to disturb our deep peace and that immutable calm which alone lets the divine forces manifest through us without any deformation.

O Lord, my prayer is not formulated, but Thou hearest it.

December 12, 1914

WE must know at each moment how to lose everything that we may gain everything; we must be able to shed the past like a dead body that we may be reborn into a greater plenitude. . . . It is so that the constant aspiration of the inner being expresses itself; turned to Thee, it wants to reflect Thee in an ever purer mirror; and Thy unchanging Beatitude is translated in it into a propelling force of progress of an incomparable intensity; and this force is transformed in the most external being into a calm and assured will which no obstacle can vanquish.

O divine Master, with what an ardent love I serve Thee! With what a pure, still and infinite joy I am Thyself in all that is and beyond all existence in form.

And the two consciousnesses unite in an unequalled plenitude.

December 15, 1914

O LORD, Thou hast given me peace in power, serenity in action, immutable happiness in the heart of all circumstances.

December 22, 1914

IT is for the Truth, O Lord, that I implore Thee.

Once again make active this mind which fell mute in order to surrender to Thee, give it the knowledge of Thy will.

It welcomed and allowed all possibilities to take form in it; then in order to stop the conflict of their contrary tendencies, it closed the door to these unwelcome visitors, saying: "I don't need to live actively, to know what Thy will is, Lord, provided that I can transmit the ray of Thy eternal light without distorting it." So it was done and the will became submissive, one-pointed, precise and strong. But now Thou wouldst have the mind know, and Thou hast said to it: "Awake and become aware of the Truth." Then the mind has answered with joy, and now it turns to the resplendent sun of sovereign Truth, calling it to itself in order to manifest it.

Thou wouldst break down all barriers, one after another, that the being may take on the integral amplitude of all its possibilities of manifestation.

Let all earthly desires come together in me, O Lord, so that Thou mayst consider them, and Thy will be able to work precisely, clearly, definitively upon the smallest detail as upon the whole.

Thus the advent of the awaited time will be hastened. . . .

All the being exults in intense joy and unequalled plenitude.

January 2, 1915

EVERY idea, however powerful and profound it may be, repeated too often, expressed too constantly, becomes stale, insipid, worthless. . . . The highest concepts thus lose their freshness after a time and the intelligence which delighted in transcendental speculations suddenly feels an imperious need to abandon all reasonings and all its philosophy and contemplate life with the marvelling gaze of a child, so as no longer to remember anything of its past knowledge, were it even a sovereignly divine one. . . .

It is true to say that the divisions of time are purely arbitrary, that the date assigned to the renewal of the year varies according to the latitude, the climate, the customs, and that it is purely conventional. This is the mental attitude which smiles at the childishness of men and wants to let itself be guided by profounder truths. And then suddenly the mind itself feels its powerlessness to translate these truths precisely, and, renouncing all wisdom of this kind, it lets the song of the aspiring heart arise, the heart for which every circumstance is an opportunity for a deeper, vaster and more intense aspiration. . . . The year of the West renews itself: why not profit by it to will with renewed ardour that this symbol should become a reality and the deplorable things of the past give place to things which must exist in all glory?

Always we believe that we can define Thee, can shut Thee up in our mental formulas; but however vast, complex, synthetic they may be, Thou wilt remain always the Inexpressible even for him who knows and lives Thee. . . .

For one can live Thee though one is unable to express Thee, can be Thy infinity and realise it though unable to define or explain Thee; always Thou wilt remain the eternal mystery, worthy of all our wonder; — not only in Thy unthinkable and even unknowable Transcendence but in Thy universal manifestation, in all that we integrally are. And always forms of thought are succeeded by new forms, ever purer, higher and more comprehensive, but never will one of them be considered sufficient to give so much as an idea of what Thou art. And each new fact will be a new problem, more marvellous and mysterious than all that preceded it. Yet, faced with its own ignorance and incapacity, the mental being remains luminous, smiling and calm, even as though it possessed the supreme knowledge — that of its being Thou, innumerably, invariably, infinitely, very simply Thou.

January 11, 1915

MORE than ever before, the aspiration of the mental being rose to Thee with great fervour. . . . The perception of infinity and eternity is always there. But it is as if Thou hadst willed to cut me off from all religious joy, all spiritual ecstasy, in order to plunge me into the most strictly material circumstances. Everywhere, O Lord, is Thy perfect bliss, and nothing can take away from me that grand gift Thou hast made of it to me; in every place and every circumstance it is with me, it is myself as I am Thou. But all this is nothing beside what should be. Thou wantest that from the heart of this heavy and obscure Matter I make the volcano of Thy Love and Light burst forth; Thou wantest that breaking all the old conventions of language there may arise a Word fit to express Thee, a Word never heard before; Thou wouldst that the union between the smallest things below and the vastest, sublimest things above might become integral; and that is why, O Lord, cutting me off from all religious joy and all spiritual ecstasy, depriving me of all freedom to concentrate exclusively upon Thee, Thou saidst to me, "Work like an ordinary man in the midst of ordinary people; learn to be nothing more than they in everything that manifests; participate in all their ways of life; for beyond all that they know, all that they are, thou carriest within thee the torch of the eternal splendour which does not flicker, and by associating with them this is what thou wilt bring in their midst. Dost thou need to enjoy this light, so long as it radiates to all from thee? Is it necessary for thee to feel my love vibrating in thee, so long as thou givest it? Must thou taste fully the bliss of my presence, so long as thou canst serve as its intermediary to all?

May Thy will be done, O Lord — done integrally. It is my happiness and my law.

January 17, 1915

NOW, Lord, things have changed. The time of rest and preparation is over. Thou hast willed that from the passive and contemplative servitor I was, I become an active and realising one; Thou hast willed that joyful acceptance be transformed into joyful battle, and that in a constant and heroic effort against everything which in the world opposes the accomplishment of Thy law in its purest and highest present expression, I find again the same peaceful and unchanging poise which one keeps in a surrender to Thy law as it is now being accomplished, that is, without entering into a direct struggle with all that opposes it, making the best of every circumstance and acting by contagion, example and slow infusion.

In a partial and limited battle, but one that is representative of the great terrestrial struggle, Thou dost put my strength, determination and courage to the test to see if I can truly be Thy servitor. If the result of the battle shows that I am worthy of being the mediator of Thy regenerating action, Thou wilt extend the field of action. And if I always live up to what Thou expectest of me, a day will come, O Lord, when Thou wilt be upon earth, and the whole earth will rise against Thee. But Thou wilt take the earth in Thy arms and the earth will be transformed.

January 18, 1915

LORD, hear my prayer. . . .

In me Thou art all-powerful, sovereign Master of my destiny, my life's guide, conqueror of all obstacles, victor over preconceived wills and mental prejudices. Perhaps to be all-powerful in the world outside, Thou needest the instrumentation of my mind, organiser and shaper of the means of action; but if Thou canst make the instrument perfect, how can there be any doubt that the work will be accomplished? All evil shadows which bring contrary suggestions must be driven away very far and, with a complete and unshakable trust in Thy infinite mercy, I address this prayer to Thee:

Transform Thy enemies into friends,

Change the darkness into light.

In this immense heroic struggle, in this sublime struggle of love against hatred, of justice against injustice, of obedience to Thy supreme law against revolt, may I gradually be able to make humanity worthy of a still sublimer peace in which, all internal dissensions having ceased, the whole effort of man may be united for the attainment of a more and more perfect and integral realisation of Thy divine Will and Thy progressive ideal.

January 24, 1915

LORD, I have long remained silent before Thee in one of those inner prostrations full of an ardent adoration which culminate in a supreme identification. . . . And, as always, Thou saidst to me: "Turn thy look towards the earth." And I saw all the roads wide open and radiant with a calm and pure light.

In mute adoration, filled utterly with Thy will, I turned towards the earth.

February 15, 1915 *

O LORD of Truth, thrice have I implored Thy manifestation invoking Thee with deep fervour.

Then, as always, the whole being made its total submission. At that moment the consciousness perceived the individual being mental, vital and physical, covered all over with dust, and this being lay prostrate before Thee, its forehead touching the earth, dust in the dust, and it cried to Thee, "O Lord, this being made of dust prostrates itself before Thee praying to be consumed with the fire of the Truth that it may henceforth manifest only Thee." Then Thou saidst to it, "Arise, thou art pure of all that is dust." And suddenly, in a stroke, all the dust sank from it like a cloak that falls on the earth, and the being appeared erect, always as substantial but resplendent with a dazzling light.

March 3, 1915:
On board the Kamo Maru

SOLITUDE, a harsh, intense solitude, and always this strong impression of having been flung headlong into a hell of darkness! Never at any moment of my life, in any circumstances, have I felt myself living in surroundings so entirely opposite to all that I am conscious of as true, so contrary to all that is the essence of my life. Sometimes when the impression and the contrast grow very intense, I cannot prevent my total submission from taking on a hue of melancholy, and the calm and mute converse with the Master within is transformed for a moment into an invocation that almost supplicates, "O Lord, what have I done that Thou hast thrown me thus into the sombre Night?" But immediately the aspiration rises, still more ardent, "Spare this being all weakness; suffer it to be the docile and clear-eyed instrument of Thy work, whatever that work may be."

For the moment the clear-sightedness is lacking; never was the future more veiled. It is as though we were moving towards a high, impenetrable wall, so far as the destiny of individual men is concerned. As for the destinies of nations and of the earth, they appear more distinctly. But of these it is useless to speak: the future will reveal them clearly to all eyes, even of the most blind.

March 4, 1915

ALWAYS the same harsh solitude ... but it is not painful, on the contrary. In it more clearly than ever, is revealed the pure and infinite love in which the whole earth is immersed. By this love all lives and is animated; the darkest shadows become almost translucent to let its streams flow through, and the intensest pain is transformed into potent bliss.

Each turn of the propeller upon the deep ocean seems to drag me farther away from my true destiny, the one best expressing the divine Will; each passing hour seems to plunge me again deeper into that past with which I had broken, sure of being called to new and vaster re-alisations; everything seems to draw me back to a state of things totally contrary to the life of my soul which reigns uncontested over outer activities; and, despite the apparent sadness of my own situation, the consciousness is so firmly established in a world which passes beyond personal limitations on every side, that the whole being rejoices in a constant perception of power and love.

In the material actuality, tomorrow lies dark and un-readable; no light, not even the faintest, reveals to my be-wildered gaze any indication, any presence of the Divine. But something in the depths of consciousness turns to the Invisible and Sovereign Witness and tells him: "Thou dost plunge me, O Lord, into the thickest darkness; this means that Thou hast established Thy light so firmly in me that Thou knowest it will stand this perilous ordeal. Otherwise wouldst Thou have chosen me for the descent

295

into the vortex of this hell as Thy torch-bearer? Wouldst Thou have judged my heart strong enough not to fail, my hand firm enough not to tremble? And yet my individual being knows how weak and powerless it is; when Thou dost not manifest Thy Presence, it is more denuded than most people who do not know or care for Thee. In Thee alone lies its strength and ability. If Thou art pleased to make use of it, nothing will be too difficult to accomplish, no task too vast and complex. But if Thou shouldst withdraw, just a poor child is left, capable only of nestling in Thy arms and sleeping there in the sweet dreamless sleep where nothing else exists but Thou."

March 7, 1915

IT is past, the time of sweet mental silence, so peaceful, so pure, through which could be felt the profound will expressing itself in its all-powerful truth. Now the will is no longer perceived; and the mind once more necessarily active, analyses, classifies, judges, chooses, constantly reacts as a transforming agent upon everything that is imposed on the individuality, grown wide enough to be in contact with a world infinitely vast and complex, a world of mingled light and shadow like all that belongs to the earth. *I am exiled from every spiritual happiness, and of all ordeals this, O Lord, is surely the most painful that Thou canst impose: but most of all the withdrawal of Thy will which seems to be a sign of total disapprobation. Strong is the growing sense of rejection, and it needs all the ardour of an untiring faith to keep the external consciousness thus abandoned to itself from being invaded by an irremediable sorrow. . . .

*But it refuses to despair, it refuses to believe that the misfortune is irreparable; it waits with humility in an obscure and hidden effort and struggle for the breath of Thy perfect joy to penetrate it again. And perhaps each of its modest and secret victories is a true help brought to the earth. . . .

*If it were possible to come definitively out of this external consciousness, to take refuge in the divine consciousness! But that Thou hast forbidden and still and always Thou forbidst it. No flight out of the world! The burden of its darkness and ugliness must be borne to the

297

end even if all divine succour seems to be withdrawn. I must remain in the bosom of the Night and walk on without compass, without beacon-light, without inner guide.

I will not even implore Thy mercy; for what Thou willst for me, I too will. All my energy is in tension solely to advance, always to advance step after step, despite the depth of the darkness, despite the obstacles of the way, and whatever comes, O Lord, it is with a fervent and unchanging love that Thy decision will be welcomed. Even if Thou findest the instrument unfit to serve Thee, the instrument belongs to itself no more, it is Thine; Thou canst destroy or magnify it, it exists not in itself, it wills nothing, it can do nothing without Thee.

298

March 8, 1915 *

FOR the most part the condition is one of calm and profound indifference; the being feels neither desire nor repulsion, neither enthusiasm nor depression, neither joy nor sorrow. It regards life as a spectacle in which it takes only a very small part; it perceives its actions and reactions, conflicts and forces as things that at once belong to its own existence which overflows the small personality on every side and yet to that personality are altogether foreign and remote.

But from time to time a great breath passes, a great breath of sorrow, of anguished isolation, of spiritual destitution, — one might almost say, the despairing appeal of Earth abandoned by the Divine. It is a pang as silent as it is cruel, a sorrow submissive, without revolt, without any desire to avoid or pass out of it and full of an infinite sweetness in which suffering and felicity are closely wedded, something infinitely vast, great and deep, too great, too deep perhaps to be understood by men — something that holds in it the seed of To-morrow. . . .

Lunel: April 19, 1915

AN imperious need has forced me to return to this confidant of my seekings and the efforts of my soul.

All external circumstances have changed, giving a flat lie to the dream of the ideal which sought expression even in material activities. The hour has not yet come for joyful realisations in outer physical things. The physical being is plunged once again into the dull, monotonous night from which it wanted to withdraw too hastily; and Thy realised will, O Lord of Truth, has come to tell the constructing mind: "You don't think this is true, and yet it *is*." The mind has readily recognised that it was mistaken and has surrendered completely to all that Thou willest. The vital being is quiet and satisfied in all circumstances. All feeling dwells in an equal and pure peace; the whole being is flooded with Thy vast, eternal light; Thy love penetrates and animates it. And yet the impression that outer facts are a falsehood has not been effaced, and the body, despite its indisputable goodwill, is so profoundly shaken that it cannot manage to regain its equilibrium and health.

The entire earthly life of this being, from its very beginning to the present moment, gives it the impression of an unreal dream, very remote from it, having almost no further contact with it; all this outer mechanism is now only a machine which it moves, for such is the will of its central Reality, but it is no longer interested in it, perhaps sometimes even less than the neighbouring mechanism or even the unknown mechanism that will be the product

300

of the earth of tomorrow. But this earth itself is strange to it, and as it is not aware of anything else except the Eternal Silence, all life that has form appears remote and almost unreal to it; it seems strange to it that anyone could desire anything since it does not exist, or prefer one thing to another since neither is there. But at the same time it does not see why it should object to any action whatever it may be, since all actions are equally unreal, and it does not feel the necessity to flee from a world which does not exist and cannot be a burden, since its existence is so inexistent.

All this gives the feeling of a sort of void full of light, peace, immensity, eluding all form and all definition. It is the Nought, but a Nought which is real and can last eternally, for it *is*, even while having the perfect immensity of that which is not. . . . Poor words which try to say what silence itself cannot express.

The condition thus trying to define itself in awkward terms gradually settled in some weeks ago, and every passing day establishes it more definitively, more deeply, more irremediably so to speak. Without having wanted it, sought for it or desired it, the being sinks deeper and deeper into it, also gradually losing consciousness of itself in a Consciousness which is no longer individual and whose immobility is inexpressible — a Consciousness from which it is no longer possible to distinguish oneself.

May 24, 1915

ONE day, O Lord, Thou didst teach my mind that it could act fully as an instrument of manifestation of Thy divine truth, as an intermediary of Thy eternal will, without being limited in its realising constructions by the narrow field of possibilities of the external being. Till then this mind, except very rarely, was in the habit of coming out of its mute ecstasy, its silent contemplation before Thy ineffable infinity, only to concentrate its effort on the centre of action represented by the external being; and this was a sort of bondage within too narrow a frame; there was a contradiction between the powers of mental realisation and the instrument through which they were striving to make their way out; the most immediate result was the wastage and limitation of mental energies, which not finding any satisfaction in activity, quite naturally returned to merge into Thy eternity.

Suddenly Thou didst put an end to this disorder; Thou didst liberate the mind from its last fetters; Thou didst teach it to be freely active through all forms and no longer exclusively through those it considered till then as its own, that is, as its natural means of expression.

The vital being had already realised this liberation long ago and knew how to enjoy the plenitude of sensations and emotions in all forms capable of manifesting life. But the mental being had not yet learnt how to animate, organise and illuminate consciously all lives without distinction. Thou didst break down all barriers, Thou didst open to it the doors of Thy infinite manifestation.

Within a few days the new conquest was established, affirmed. And what Thou expectest from the centre of consciousness represented at present upon earth by my whole being, grew clear before it: To be the life in all material forms, the thought organising and using this life in all forms, the love widening, enlightening, intensifying, uniting all the varied elements of this thought, and thus, through a total identification with the manifested world, to be able to intervene with full power in its transformations.

On the other hand, by a perfect surrender to the Supreme Principle, to become aware of the Truth and the eternal Will that manifests it. Through this identification having become the faithful servant and sure intermediary of the divine Will, and uniting this conscious identification with the Principle to the conscious identification with its becoming, to mould and model consciously the love, mind and life of the becoming in accordance with the Law of Truth of the Principle.

This is how the individual being can be the conscious mediator between the absolute Truth and the manifested universe and intervene in the slow, uncertain march of the Yoga of Nature in order to give it the swiftness, intensity and sureness of the divine Yoga.

This is how in certain periods the entire terrestrial life seems to cross miraculously over stages which at other times would require thousands of years to traverse.

At present, O Lord, the state of perfect and conscious

303

surrender to Thy eternal will is, as far as I can tell, constant, invariable behind every act, every movement of the mind, the vital or the body. This imperturbable calm, this deep, peaceful, unchanging bliss, which never leave me — are they not a proof of this?

Passive or receptive identification with life, thought and love in all manifested forms is an accomplished fact, apparently the inevitable consequence of surrender to pure Truth.

But the moments when consciousness becomes effectively the life animating and moulding all material forms, the intelligence organising life, and the love illuminating the intelligence, in an active and fully conscious way, at once in the totality and the least detail, with a sense of infinite plenitude and precise powers — these moments are still intermittent though growing more and more frequent and lasting.

It is in these moments that the two consciousnesses are simultaneous and fuse into a single, almost indescribable, ineffable consciousness in which are united Immutable Eternity and Eternal Movement. It is in these moments that the present work begins to be accomplished.

Marsillargues: July 31, 1915

SHOULD I, playing the role of a servant, an instrument, turn to Thee, O Lord, and address a hymn of adoration to Thee? Should I, identifying myself with Thee in the eternal Reality and infinite Bliss, speak to men of the peace and joy they do not know? ... The two attitudes are simultaneous, the two consciousnesses parallel, and in this close and indissoluble union lies Plenitude.

The heavens are definitively conquered, and nothing and nobody could have the power of wresting them from me. But the conquest of the earth is still to be made; it is being carried on in the very heart of the turmoil; and even when achieved, it will still be only a relative one; the victories in this world are but stages leading progressively to still more glorious victories; and what Thy Will makes my mind conceive of as the goal to be attained, the conquest to be realised, is only one element of Thy eternal plan; but in perfect union I am this plan and this Will, and I taste the supreme bliss of the infinite, even while playing ardently, with precision and energy, in the world of division, the special part Thou hast entrusted to me.

Thy power in me is like a living spring, strong and abundant, rumbling behind the rocks, gathering its energies to break down the obstacles and gush out freely in the open, pouring its waters over the plain to fertilise it. When will the hour of this emergence come? When the moment arrives, it will burst forth, and time is nothing in Eternity. But what words can describe the immensity of joy brought by this inner accumulation, this deep concentration, of all the forces that are submissive to the manifestation of Thy Will of tomorrow, preparing to break over the world, drowning in their sovereign flood all that still persists in wanting to be the expression of Thy will of yesterday, so as to take possession of the earth in Thy Name and offer it to Thee as a completer image of Thyself.

Thou hast said that the earth would die, and it will die to its old ignorance.

Thou hast said that the earth would live, and it will live in the renewal of Thy Power.

What words will ever tell the splendour of Thy Law and the magnificence of Thy Glory? What words will express the perfection of Thy Consciousness and the infinite bliss of Thy Love?

What words will sing Thy ineffable Peace and celebrate the majesty of Thy Silence and the grandeur of Thy all-powerful Truth?

The entire manifested universe cannot suffice to speak Thy splendour and tell Thy marvels, and in the eternity of time this is what it is trying to do more and more, better and better, eternally.

Paris: November 2, 1915

(After a few moments spent in arranging familiar objects)

AS a strong breeze passes over the sea and crowns with foam its countless waves, so a great breath passed over the memory and awoke the multitude of its remembrances. Intense, complex, crowded, the past lived again in a flash, having lost nothing of its savour, its richness.

Then was the whole being lifted up in a great surge of adoration, and gathering all its memories like an abundant harvest, it placed them at Thy feet, O Lord, as an offering.

For throughout its life, without knowing it or with some presentiment of it, it was Thou whom it was seeking; in all its passions, all its enthusiasms, all its hopes and disillusionments, all its sufferings and all its joys, it was Thou whom it ardently wanted. And now that it has found Thee, now that it possesses Thee in a supreme Peace and Felicity, it wonders that it should have needed so many sensations, emotions, experiences to discover Thee.

But all this, which was a struggle, a turmoil, a perpetual effort, has become through the sovereign grace of Thy conscious Presence, a priceless fortune which the being rejoices to offer as its gift to Thee. The purifying flame of Thy illumination has turned it into jewels of price laid down as a living holocaust on the altar of my heart.

307

Errors have become stepping-stones, the blind gropings conquests. Thy glory transforms defeats into victories of eternity, and all the shadows have fled before Thy radiant light.

It is Thou who wert the motive and the goal; Thou art the worker and the work.

The personal existence is a canticle, perpetually renewed, which the universe offers up to Thy inconceivable Splendour.

November 7, 1915. 3 a.m.

Without any external sign, any special circumstance, the moments passed by so majestically, in so solemn an inner silence, a calm so deep and vast, that my tears began to flow profusely. For the last two days the earth seems to have been going through a decisive crisis; it seems that the great formidable contest between material resistances and spiritual powers is nearing its conclusion, or, in any case, that some element of capital importance has made or is going to make its appearance in the play.

How little do individual beings count at such times! They are like wisps of straw carried away by the passing breeze, whirling for a moment above the ground, only to be flung back upon it again and reduced to dust. And individual beings who thus feel so insecure, so stripped of importance, suffer and groan in painful agony. For them the waiting itself is a perpetual menace, everything speaks of danger and destruction. . . .

But what grandeur, what sovereign beauty lie in the depth of this outer anguish all formed of narrow egoism; what splendour dwells within this waiting, grown sacred through deep contemplation, when the walls of personal blindness have fallen and the individual consciousness has taken its flight into immensity to unite with Thy eternal consciousness.

This sorrowful world kneels before Thee, O Lord, in mute supplication; Matter, tortured, takes shelter at Thy feet, its last and only refuge; and imploring Thee thus, it adores Thee, Thee whom it neither knows nor understands! Its prayer rises like the cry of one in a last agony; what is disappearing feels vaguely the possibility of living once again in Thee; the earth awaits Thy decree in a grandiose prostration. Listen, listen: its voice implores and supplicates to Thee. . . . What will be Thy decree, what is Thy sentence? O Lord of Truth, this individual world blesses Thy truth which it does not yet know, but which it calls, and to which it adheres with all the joyful energy of its living forces.

Death has passed, vast and solemn, and all was hushed in a religious silence while it was passing by.

A superhuman beauty has appeared upon earth.

Something more marvellous than the most marvellous bliss has brought a foretaste of its Presence.

November 26, 1915 *

THE entire consciousness immersed in divine contemplation, the whole being enjoyed a supreme and vast felicity.

Then was the physical body seized, first in its lower members and next the whole of it, by a sacred trembling which made all personal limits fall away little by little even in the most material sensation. The being grew in greatness progressively, methodically, breaking down every barrier, shattering every obstacle, that it might contain and manifest a force and a power which increased ceaselessly in immensity and intensity. It was as a progressive dilatation of the cells until there was a complete identification with the earth: the body of the awakened consciousness was the terrestrial globe moving harmoniously in ethereal space. And the consciousness knew that its global body was thus moving in the arms of the universal Being, and it gave itself, it abandoned itself to It in an ecstasy of peaceful bliss. Then it felt that its body was absorbed in the body of the universe and one with it; the consciousness became the consciousness of the universe, immobile in its totality, moving infinitely in its internal complexity. The consciousness of the universe sprang towards the Divine in an ardent aspiration, a perfect surrender, and it saw in the splendour of the immaculate Light the radiant Being standing on a many-headed serpent whose body coiled infinitely around the universe. The Being in an eternal gesture of triumph mastered and created at one and the same time the serpent and the universe that issued from

311

him; erect on the serpent he dominated it with all his victorious might, and the same gesture that crushed the hydra enveloping the universe gave it eternal birth. Then the consciousness became this Being and perceived that its form was changing once more; it was absorbed into something which was no longer a form and yet contained all forms, something which, immutable, sees, — the Eye, the Witness. And what It sees, is. Then this last vestige of form disappeared and the consciousness itself was absorbed into the Unutterable, the Ineffable.

The return towards the consciousness of the individual body took place very slowly in a constant and invariable splendour of Light and Power and Felicity and Adoration, by successive gradations, but directly, without passing again through the universal and terrestrial forms. And it was as if the modest corporeal form had become the direct and immediate vesture, without any intermediary, of the supreme and eternal Witness.[1]

---

[1] This is a letter which the Mother sent to Sri Aurobindo and to which he answered on 31-12-1915 as follows:

The experience you have described is Vedic in the real sense, though not one which would easily be recognised by the modern systems of Yoga which call themselves Vedic. It is the union of the "Earth" of the Veda and Purana with the divine Principle, an earth which is said to be above our earth, that is to say, the physical being and consciousness of which the world and the body are only images. But the modern Yogas hardly recognise the possibility of a material union with the Divine.

312

January 15, 1916

O THOU whom I may call my God, Thou who art the personal form of the Transcendent Eternal, the Cause, Source and Reality of my individual being, Thou who hast through the centuries and millenniums slowly and subtly kneaded this Matter, so that one day it could become consciously identified with Thee, and be nothing but Thee; O Thou who hast appeared to me in all Thy divine splendour — this individual being in all its complexity offers itself to Thee in an act of supreme adoration; it aspires in its entirety to be identified with Thee, to be Thyself, eternally Thou, merged for ever in Thy Reality. But is it ready for that? Is Thy work fully accomplished? Is there in it no longer any shadow, ignorance, or limitation? Canst Thou at last definitively take possession of it and, in the sublimest, most integral transformation free it forever from the world of Ignorance and make it live in the world of Truth?

Or rather Thou art myself divested of all error and limitation. Have I become integrally this true self in all the atoms of my being? Wilt Thou bring about an overwhelming transformation, or will it still be a slow action in which cell after cell must be wrested from its darkness and its limits? . . .

Thou art the Sovereign, ready to take possession of Thy kingdom; dost Thou not find Thy kingdom yet ready enough for Thee to link it definitively to Thyself and become integrated with it?

Will the great miracle of the integral Divine Life in the individual at last be accomplished?

January 22, 1916

THOU hast taken entire possession of this miserable instrument and if it is not yet perfected enough for Thee to complete its transformation, its transmutation, Thou art at work in each one of its cells to knead it and make it supple and enlighten it, and in the whole being, to arrange, organise and harmonise it. Everything is in movement, everything is changing; Thy divine action makes itself felt as an ineffable spring of a purifying fire that circulates through all the atoms. And this flowing spring has brought into the being an ecstasy more marvellous than any it had ever felt before: thus to Thy action there answers the aspiration of that on which Thou workest and the aspiration is all the more ardent because the instrument has seen itself as it really is in all its infirmity.

O Lord, I implore Thee, hasten the blessed day when the divine miracle will be accomplished, hasten the day of the realisation of the Divine upon earth.

January 23, 1916

O THOU divine inhabitant of this gross form, Thou
seest that it is a mass of limitations: wilt Thou not break
all these limitations so that it may participate in Thy
infinity? Thou seest that it is full of obscurities: wilt Thou
not dissolve this darkness with Thy resplendent light so
that it may participate in Thy brightness? Thou seest it
burdened with ignorant impurities: wilt Thou not consume all these impurities with Thy devouring fire of love,
so that the being in its integrality may now become one
in all consciousness with Thee?

Dost Thou not find that this sombre and sorrowful
experience of egoistic separativity has lasted long enough
for the earth and humanity? Has not the hour struck in
the universe for this phase of development to be replaced
by another, dominated by the pure and vast consciousness
of Thy Unity?

Unceasingly, at every moment, my invocation rises to
Thee, and I call Thee: Lord, O Lord, take possession of
Thy kingdom, illumine it with Thy eternal Presence, put
an end to the cruel error in which it lives believing itself
separate from Thee, while in its reality and essence it is
Thyself.

Break, break down the last resistances, consume the
last impurities, blast this being if need be, but let it be
transfigured!

Tokio: *June 7, 1916*

LONG months have gone by in which nothing could be said, for it was a period of transition, of passing from one equilibrium to another, vaster and more complete. The outer circumstances were manifold and new, as if the being needed to accumulate many perceptions and observations in order to give a more extensive and complex base to its experience. But, being entirely plunged within this experience, it did not have the necessary perspective to see it as a whole, to know what it was and above all where it was leading.

Suddenly, on the fifth of June the veil was rent, and there was light in my consciousness.

When I contemplated Thee in Thy individual form, O Lord of eternity, and implored Thee to take possession of Thy kingdom of the flesh, Thou didst set again into motion, into activity this vital form, which, for the necessity of development and unification, had been living for years in a passivity that was receptive and harmonious but alien to all active manifestation of Thy will.

This return to activity meant a completely new adaptation of the vital instrument, for its natural tendency is always to resume action with its old habits and methods. This period of adaptation was long, painful, sometimes obscure, though behind, the perception of Thy Presence and perfect surrender to Thy Law were immutable and quite strongly conscious for any disturbance to shake the being.

Gradually the vital being grew accustomed to find

317

harmony in the intensest action as it had in passive surrender. And once this harmony was sufficiently established, there was light again in all the parts of the being, and the consciousness of what had happened became complete.

Now in the heart of action the vital being has discovered the perception of Infinity and Eternity. It can perceive Thy Supreme Beauty and live it in all sensations and all forms. Even in its every sensation, extended, active, fully developed to feel contrary sensations at the same time, always it perceives Thee.

It is not unaware, however, that this is only one stage, and it bows before Thee in a profound adoration and tells Thee: "Lord, Thou hast taken up Thy instrument again and willed to use it for action. The instrument knows its imperfection and impurity and implores Thy mercy to perfect and purify it, so that, day by day, through a progressive disappearance of all its preferences and limitations, it may be able to manifest Thee more integrally."

November 28, 1916

THOU madest me read these childish babblings once
again, for they are awkward attempts at expression of a
mind still in its infancy and all this seemed to me far, very
remote, clad in the charm and purity of the experiences
of a candid and enthusiastic childhood. And yet, before
Thee, O eternal Lord, I have not grown any older and
have not made any progress; the expression of today will
not be better than that of those early days. The mind
is still as poor and clumsy as before. And what could
it have to express that is so remarkable? No sensational
experience: all experiences now seem simple and natural.
No powerful or exceptional new idea, none of those ideas
which fill one with the joy of discovery: all ideas, whatever
form they may take, now seem like old acquaintances one
greets amicably in passing, but from whom one expects
nothing new. No scrupulous and detailed psychological
analysis, exposing some yet unexplored inner recess: internal complications no longer exist in themselves; they
are faithful and impartial reflections of all the surround-
ing psychological movements; and to describe what is
going on in the being would be at once as complicated
and monotonous as to describe the world in its almost
exclusively subsconscient gropings and wanderings.

Poverty, poverty! Thou hast placed me in an arid and
bare desert and yet this desert is sweet to me as everything that comes from Thee, O Lord. In this dull and
wan greyness, in this dim ashen light, I taste the savour
of the infinite spaces: the pure breeze of the open seas,

319

the powerful breath of the free heights constantly fill my heart and penetrate my life; all barriers have fallen, within and around me, and I feel like a bird opening its wings for an unrestrained flight. But the bird remains perched upon a rock, its wings outspread against the grey, fleecy sky, awaiting, in order to soar upwards, the coming of something it expects without knowing what it is. As it no longer has any chains to check its flight, it no longer dreams of flying away. Conscious of its freedom, it does not enjoy it, and remains like the others, among the others, perched on the ground in the midst of the dark and dense fog.

December 4, 1916

SINCE Thou hast permitted it, O Lord, I have once again begun to come to Thee daily, freeing myself for a few brief moments from an activity of which I know the complete relativity, even while I am engaged in it. Thou hadst plunged me back into action and the ordinary consciousness, and now Thou grantest me the possibility of regularly taking my flight again to Thee, to soar awhile in the immutable Silence and eternal Consciousness.

Thou hast willed, O Lord, that the being should grow wider and richer. It could not do so without entering once again, at least partially and temporarily, into ignorance and obscurity.

This ignorance and obscurity it comes now to lay at Thy feet as the most humble of ordeals. I shall not ask Thee to bestow upon me continuously the Consciousness Thou grantest me in these moments of peaceful and pure communion. I shall ask Thee only to make these moments still more peaceful and pure, to fortify and enlighten the consciousness more and more, so that it may return to its daily task with renewed strength and knowledge.

Thou remindest me through these brief moments of ecstatic identification that Thou hast granted me the power of consciously uniting with Thee. And the divine musical harmony captures the entire being.

But the sounds gather in the head as behind a veil and not a word flows from the pen today. . . .

321

December 5, 1916

THOU hast granted me the grace of Thy repose in which all individual limits are dissolved, in which one is in all and, more clearly still, all is in oneself. But the mind, merged in this divine ecstasy, cannot yet find any power of expression.

(*Factual notation of the experience*)

"Turn towards the earth." The usual injunction was heard in the silence of the immutable identification. Then the consciousness became that of the One in all. "Everywhere and in all those in whom thou canst see the One, there will awake the consciousness of this identity with the Divine. Look. . . . " It was a Japanese street brilliantly illuminated by gay lanterns picturesquely adorned with vivid colours. And as gradually what was conscious moved on down the street, the Divine appeared, visible in everyone and everything. One of the lightly-built houses became transparent, revealing a woman seated on a tatami in a sumptuous violet kimono embroidered with gold and bright colours. The woman was beautiful and must have been between thirty-five and forty. She was playing a golden samisen. At her feet lay a little child. And in the woman too the Divine was visible.

December 7, 1916

LORD, I could in truth say that I have neither Yoga nor any virtues, for I am completely divested of that which constitutes the glory of all those who want to serve Thee. Apparently my life is as ordinary and banal as can be; and inwardly what is it? Nothing but a calm tranquillity without any variation or surprises; the calm of a something which has realised and no longer seeks itself, which no longer expects anything from life and things, which acts without reckoning upon any profit, knowing perfectly that this action does not belong to it in any way, either in its impulsion or in its result; which wills, being aware that the supreme Will alone wills in it; a calm all made of an incontestable certitude, an objectless knowledge, a causeless joy, a self-existent state of consciousness which no longer belongs to time. It is an immobility moving in the domain of external life, yet without belonging to it or seeking to escape from it. I hope for nothing, expect nothing, desire nothing, aspire for nothing and, above all, I am nothing; and yet happiness, a calm, unmixed happiness, a happiness unaware of itself, which does not need to look at its own being, has come to dwell in the house of this body. This happiness is Thou, O Lord, and this calm is Thou, Lord, for these are not human faculties and men's senses can neither appreciate nor enjoy them. Thus it is Thou, O Lord, who dwellest in this body, and that is why this corporeal abode seems so poor and drab for so marvellous an occupant.

December 8, 1916

THIS was our conversation today morning, O Lord:
Thou didst wake up the vital being with the magic wand of Thy impulsion and say to it: "Awake, bend the bow of thy will, for soon the hour of action will come." Suddenly awakened, the vital being rose up, stretched itself and shook off the dust of its long torpidity; from the elasticity of its members it realised that it was still vigorous and fit for action. And with an ardent faith it answered the sovereign call: "Here I am, what dost Thou want of me, O Lord?" But before another word could be pronounced, the mind intervened in its turn and, having bowed down to the Master as a mark of obedience, spoke to him thus: "Thou knowest, O Lord, that I am surrendered to Thee and that I try my best to be a faithful and pure intermediary of Thy supreme Will. But when I turn my gaze to the earth, I see that however great men may be, their field of action is always terribly restricted. A man, who in his mind and even in his vital being is as vast as the universe or at least as vast as the earth, as soon as he begins to act, becomes enclosed in the narrow bounds of a material action, very limited in its field and results. Whether he be the founder of a religion or a political reformer, he who acts becomes a petty little stone in the general edifice, a grain of sand in the immense dune of human activities. So I do not see any realisable action worthy of the whole being's concentrating on it and making it its purpose of existence. The vital being delights in adventure; but should it be allowed to fling

324

itself into some lamentable adventure unworthy of an instrument conscious of Thy Presence?" — "Fear nothing," was the reply. "The vital being will not be allowed to set itself in motion, it will not be asked of thee to contribute all the effort of thy organising faculties, except when the action proposed is vast and complete enough to fully and usefully employ all the qualities of the being. What exactly this action will be, thou wilt know when it comes to thee. But I am warning thee even now so that thou mayst be prepared not to reject it. I also warn both thee and the vital being that the time for the small, quiet, uniform and peaceful life will be over. There will be effort, danger, the unforeseen, insecurity, but also intensity. Thou wert made for this role. After having accepted for long years to forget it completely, because the time had not come and thou too wert not ready, wake up now to the consciousness that this is indeed thy true role, that it was for this thou wert created."

The vital being was the first to awake to consciousness and, with the enthusiasm natural to it, exclaimed: "I am ready, O Lord, Thou mayst rely upon me!" The mind, weaker and more timid, though more docile too, added: "What Thou willest, I will. Thou knowest well, O Lord, that I belong entirely to Thee. But shall I be able to prove equal to the task, shall I have the power of organising what the vital being has the capacity to realise?" — "It is to prepare thee for this that I am working at the moment; this is why thou art undergoing a discipline of plasticity and enrichment. Do not worry about anything: power comes with the need. Not because thou hast been confined, even as the vital being, to very small activities at a time when this was useful, to allow things which had to be prepared the time for preparation — not because of this, I say, art thou incapable of living outside these smallnesses in a field of action consonant with thy true stature. I have appointed thee from all eternity to be my exceptional representative upon the earth, not only invisibly, in a hidden way, but also openly before the eyes of all men. And what thou wert created to be, thou wilt be."

As always, Lord, when the voice of the depths fell silent, Thy sublime and all-powerful benediction enveloped me completely.

And for a moment the Master and the instrument were but one: the Unique, eternal, infinite.

December 9, 1916

IT is now, a long while after having come out of my contemplation, that I realise what it was.

Once again this evening I entered that state in which the consciousness is scattered in a multitude of different elements, centres of consciousness both individual and collective, to carry out a certain action there or rather as many actions as these elements comprise.

By flashes one point or another suddenly appears distinctly, then fades away giving place to another. Each element of consciousness that acts is clearly conscious of its action; but a consciousness of the whole seems to be both impossible because of the extreme complexity it would entail and useless for the accomplishment of the work itself.

327

December 10, 1916

CERTAIN apparent weaknesses are sometimes more useful to Thee for Thy work, O Lord, than too evident a perfection. A manifest perfection seems to be the possible prerogative only of one who has withdrawn both from the world and from work in the world. But for him whom Thou hast chosen as one of Thy workers upon earth, I see clearly that certain weaknesses, imperfections (provided they are only apparent and not real), are in Thy eyes more useful, and hence more perfect than perfection itself. And to renounce perfection in its apparent form is part of an integral renunciation of the ignorance of the separate self.

Is that why, O Lord, Thou givest me only so rarely the ecstasy of complete identification and perfect consciousness?

I was spoiled by Thee formerly: Thou madest me live so constantly in Thy Presence. . . . But now it seems that Thou wouldst teach me to know the unchanging bliss even in darkness, and not to have any preference for either consciousness or unconsciousness.

Beyond all desire, to be plunged in the condition of those who live by desire . . . strange!

But the strangest thing is that this leaves me perfectly calm, peaceful and content, and that in this darkness I see a great strength, and that in the depth of the night sublime celestial harmonies can also be heard.

Each new step in Thy kingdom, O Lord, is a new cause for wonder!

December 12, 1916

My mind was worried about being so constantly turned towards such petty things, moving in so narrow a circle of practical and immediate thoughts.

It has learned to see Thee in everything, Lord, and in the least thing it is aware of Thee and rejoices in Thee. But even while delighting in Thee thus and recognising Thee in the most futile things and activities as well as in the vastest and noblest, it wonders why these prevail over the others. Many a time during these last months has it tried to react against this tendency but always in vain; is it because Thou findest it well thus, or because it is incapable of being otherwise? It put the question to Thee, and as always Thy smile came to comfort it; but the precise answer has not made itself heard.

Now for this mind the least object becomes an unfathomable mystery, and everything is a constantly renewed cause for wonder.

December 14, 1916

I HAIL Thee, O Lord, and bow before Thee. But I shall not write, for Thou hast just told me, in reply to a question about the present meditation: "We have had a private conversation which even thy own physical ears should not hear."

December 20, 1916

THE days have gone by, stormy and troubled to all appearance but calm and strong in their reality reflecting Thy divine will; they have gone by, deploying, disclosing, developing once more all the unexpected and varied splendour of Thy untiring divine play. And how marvellous it is to watch this when one perceives the infinite criss-crossing of the movements Thy eternal will creates, when one knows that all this is from all eternity and that it is only in our imperfect faculties that it becomes an uninterrupted succession of facts, in which we are gratuitous and ignorant actors. We act with the apparent unconsciousness and blindness of those who do not know, and yet, I do know and, even while being an actor, I am a spectator too. But I am still not pure enough for Thee to unveil before my eyes the totality of the effects and results; it is only partially and imperfectly that I know them before the act and am permitted to act with the knowledge of the "why", with a full illumination as to what Thou expectest from me. When, O Lord, shall I have this purity? But for that too I am no longer impatient and no longer implore. I see how much Thy splendours are obscured and veiled in this miserable and poor instrument; but Thou, Thou knowest why it is thus; and these its shadows and weaknesses Thou dost also use for Thy eternal ends.

My soul is in prayer and bows down in love before what it can understand and know of Thee. My soul is in prayer and gives itself unreservedly to Thee in one of

331

those sublime fervours which culminate in identification. My soul is in prayer . . . and my body too; and my thought is silent in a mute ecstasy.

(Communication received at 5.30 in the evening after meditation.)

"As thou art contemplating me, I shall speak to thee this evening. I see in thy heart a diamond surrounded by a golden light. It is at once pure and warm, something which may manifest impersonal love; but why dost thou keep this treasure enclosed in that dark casket lined with deep purple? The outermost covering is of a deep lustreless blue, a real mantle of darkness. It would seem that thou art afraid of showing thy splendour. Learn to radiate and do not fear the storm: the wind carries us far from the shore but shows us over the world. Wouldst thou be thrifty of thy tenderness? But the source of love is infinite. Dost thou fear to be misunderstood? But where hast thou seen man capable of understanding the Divine? And if the eternal truth finds in thee a means of manifesting itself, what dost thou care for all the rest? Thou art like a pilgrim coming out of the sanctuary; standing on the threshold in front of the crowd, he hesitates before revealing his precious secret, that of his supreme discovery. Listen, I too hesitated for days, for I could foresee both my preaching and its results: the imperfection of expression and the still greater imperfection of understanding. And yet I turned

332

to the earth and men and brought them my message. Turn to the earth and men — isn't this the command thou always hearest in thy heart? — in thy heart, for it is that which carries a blessed message for those who are athirst for compassion. Henceforth nothing can attack the diamond. It is unassailable in its perfect constitution and the soft radiance that flashes from it can change many things in the hearts of men. Thou doubtest thy power and fearest thy ignorance? It is precisely this that wraps up thy strength in that dark mantle of starless night. Thou hesitatest and tremblest as on the threshold of a mystery, for now the mystery of the manifestation seems to thee more terrible and unfathomable than that of the Eternal Cause. But thou must take courage again and obey the injunction from the depths. It is I who am telling thee this, for I know thee and love thee as thou didst know and love me once. I have appeared clearly before thy sight so that thou mayst in no way doubt my word. And also to thy eyes I have shown thy heart so that thou canst thus see what the supreme Truth has willed for it, so that thou mayst discover in it the law of thy being. The thing still seems to thee quite difficult: a day will come when thou wilt wonder how for so long it could have been otherwise."

Sākyamuni

333

December 21, 1916

LORD, Thou didst speak to me through the lips of one of those who have known Thee best — most probably to make me understand Thy lesson better (was I then deaf to Thy direct suggestion?). And still I do not understand at the moment what to do. Thou knowest what happiness would be mine if by Thy grace I could be integrally transformed into a hearth of divine love — that love which is the first and highest manifestation of Thy eternal Truth, that love which is at once the completest expression in this world of Thy Truth and the most direct road to lead to it the human consciousness that has gone astray. In the days when I used to aspire, desire and ask, how many times have I asked of Thee the grace of this state as the one most in conformity with my present ideal of action! And at that time it seemed to me that the day I should be purified of all egoistic preference, Thou wouldst choose this individual terrestrial being as an instrument of Thy manifestation of love upon earth. And now that Thou askest it of me, more than ever before do I feel my helplessness. For such a long time I thought I knew what love was, and now that I no longer see anything that cannot be called love, I also no longer see anything that may specially be called love. And how can I be that which I can no longer define, that state which I can no longer distinguish? And yet Thou didst show me yesterday that I was holding enclosed in a dark sheath one of Thy most precious and powerful gifts. . . . Lord, all my being aspires to obey Thy voice, to conform to Thy Law; but it does not know in its outer

334

consciousness, does not understand what Thou expectest of it. It feels indeed that at present its love is a passive state and that Thou wouldst awaken it to an active state; but how to pass from one to the other is what escapes it. It knows that this active state of love should be constant and impersonal, that is, absolutely independent of circumstances and persons, since it cannot and must not be concentrated upon any one thing in particular; and in this it will resemble the present passive state of love which is pure, unchanging and impersonal. But what it still does not know is how, even while retaining its purity, unchangeability and impersonality, qualities now inherent in its being, it can resume its activity.

That is why this evening I implored Lord Mitra who so perfectly symbolises Thy truth of love, asking him to come to my help and enlighten my ignorance, dissolve my doubts, vanquish my hesitations, break down the last obstacles and take possession of this physical instrument so that it may become what Thou expectest it to be.

But my speech is timid and my voice faltering and I do not know if Lord Mitra heard my prayer.

December 24, 1916

LORD, without allowing my mind to become aware of what was going to happen and how it was going to happen, Thou gavest me this evening a foretaste of what Thou expectest from me, only a foretaste, for it is a first, very timid step upon the marvellous road Thou hast partially opened before me. It was like a rising flood swelling, ever swelling the river until it overflows and covers everything with its beneficent waters. And this time it was the heart which thus overflowed under the pressure of the powers of love Thou didst pour into it; and the whole being began to love, to love ever more and more, without any definite aim, nothing and everything at the same time, what it knows and does not know, what it sees and has never seen; and gradually this potential love became an effective love, ready to pour itself out upon all and everything, in beneficent waves, in an active effulgence. . . . This was a beginning, a very weak beginning. But I knew, O Lord, that this is what Thou willest. As always Thy Will is an infinite Grace which floods the being with Thy divine delight and transports it far above all petty contingencies to the Glory of Thy celestial dwelling-places.

To be what Thou willest is to be divine.

December 25, 1916

(What I heard in the silence and noted down last evening)

"BY renouncing everything, even wisdom and consciousness, thou wert able to prepare thy heart for the role assigned to it: apparently the most unrewarding role, that of the spring which always lets its waters flow abundantly for all, but towards which no waters can ever run back; it draws its inexhaustible strength from the depths and expects nothing from outside. But thou canst already sense the sublime felicity that accompanies this inexhaustible expansion of love; for love is sufficient unto itself and needs no reciprocity; this is true even of individual love, how much more true then of divine love which so nobly reflects the infinite.

"Be this love in all things and everywhere, ever more widely, ever more intensely, and the whole world will become at the same time thy work and thy wealth, thy field of action and thy conquest. Fight with persistence to break down the last limits which are only frail barriers before the expansion of the being, to vanquish the last obscurities already being lit up by the Illuminating Power. Fight in order to conquer and triumph; fight to overcome everything that was till today, to make the new Light spring forth, the new Example the world needs. Fight stubbornly against all obstacles, inner or outer. It is the pearl of great price which is offered for thy Realisation."

December 26, 1916*

ALWAYS the word Thou makest me hear in the silence is sweet and encouraging, O Lord. But I see not in what this instrument is worthy of the grace Thou accordest to it or how it will have the capacity to realise what Thou attendest from it. All in it appears so small, weak and ordinary, so lacking in intensity and force and amplitude in comparison with what it should be to undertake this overwhelming role. But I know that what the mind thinks is of little importance. The mind itself knows it and, passive, it awaits the working out of Thy decree.

Thou biddest me strive without cease, and I could wish to have the indomitable ardour that prevails over every difficulty. But Thou hast put in my heart a peace so smiling that I fear I no longer know even how to strive. Things develop in me, faculties and activities, as flowers bloom, spontaneously and without effort, in a joy to be and a joy to grow, a joy to manifest Thee, whatever the mode of Thy manifestation. If struggle there is, it is so gentle and easy that it can hardly be given the name. But how small is this heart to contain so great a love! and how weak this vital and physical being to carry the power to distribute it! Thus Thou hast placed me on the threshold of the marvellous Way, but will my feet have the strength to advance upon it? . . . But Thou repliest to me that my movement is to soar and it would be an error to wish to walk. . . . O Lord, how infinite is Thy compassion! Once more

338

Thou hast taken me in Thy omnipotent arms and cradled me on Thy unfathomable heart, and Thy heart said to me, "Torment not thyself at all, be confident like a child: art thou not myself crystallised for my work?"

December 27, 1916*

O MY beloved Lord, my heart is bowed before Thee, my arms are stretched towards Thee imploring Thee to set all this being on fire with Thy sublime love that it may radiate from there on the world. My heart is wide open in my breast; my heart is open and turned towards Thee, it is open and empty that Thou mayst fill it with Thy divine Love; it is empty of all but Thee and Thy presence fills it through and through and yet leaves it empty, for it can contain also all the infinite variety of the manifested world. . . .

O Lord, my arms are outstretched in supplication towards Thee, my heart is wide open before Thee, that Thou mayst make of it a reservoir of Thy infinite love.

"Love me in all things, everywhere and in all beings" was Thy reply. I prostrate myself before Thee and ask of Thee to give me that power.

December 29, 1916*

O MY sweet Lord, teach me to be the instrument of
Thy Love.

341

December 30, 1916

WHY, O Lord, does my heart seem to me to be so cold and dry?

I feel, I see my soul living deep within my being, and my soul sees Thee, recognises Thee and loves Thee in all things, in everything that is; it is fully conscious of this, and as the outer being is surrendered to it, it too is conscious; the mind knows and never forgets; the purified vital being no longer has any attractions and repulsions, and more and more does it taste of the joy of Thy Presence in all things and always. But the heart seems to have fallen asleep in a slumber of exhaustion, and the soul no longer finds sufficient activity within it to respond fully to its impulsion. Why? Was it so poor that the struggle could thus wear it out, or so deeply wounded that it has become quite stiff? And yet it would like to answer the inner call; it wants this with a faith and ardour which have never wavered; but it is like an old man smiling benevolently at the games of youth but unable to take part in them. And yet it is full of joy and confidence, it overflows with gratitude for all the treasures of affection which Nature has so generously lavished upon it; it would like, in exchange for these precious gifts, to pour out in inexhaustible streams the golden wine of tenderness which restores and fortifies, enlivens and consoles, the true wine of life for human beings. It would like to and tries . . . but how poor is what it does beside what it dreams of doing, how mediocre what it is able to do beside what it hopes, for it hopes always. It knows that Thy call is never heard

342

in vain, and it has no doubt it can one day realise the splendours of which Thou hast given it a glimpse.

Who will open these closed flood-gates?

My heart loves in its human way, and in its human way it seems to me it loves with strength, constancy and purity. But Thou wouldst have it love divinely in a boundless unfolding of Thy sovereign power; and this remains yet unrealised for it.

Who will open these closed flood-gates? . . .

343

January 4, 1917

O LORD, Thou showerest upon me all Thy boons. Now that this being expects nothing, desires nothing from life any longer, life brings it its most precious treasures, those coveted by all men. In all the domains of my individual being Thou showerest Thy boons, in the mind, the psychic and even the physical. Thou hast placed me amidst abundance, and abundance seems to me as natural as scarcity and does not bring me a greater joy, for often in poverty the spiritual life was more intense and conscious for me; but I see this abundance very clearly, and my individual being on whom Thou heapest Thy boons thus, prostrates itself before Thee in inexpressible gratitude.

Thy goodness is unequalled and Thy mercy infinite.

January 5, 1917

LOVE is nothing but the tie that binds and holds together all the flowers of Thy divine bouquet. It is an unobtrusive role, modest, unrecognised, a role essentially impersonal, which can find all its utility only in this very impersonality.

Because I am becoming more and more this tie, this link of union gathering the scattered fragments of Thy consciousness and enabling them, by grouping them together, to reconstitute better and better Thy consciousness, at once single and multiple, it was possible for me to see clearly what love is in the play of universal forces, what its place and mission; it is not an end in itself but it is Thy supreme means. Active, everywhere, between all things, everywhere it is veiled by the very things it unites, which, though feeling its effect, are sometimes not even aware of its presence.

O Lord, Thy sweetness has entered my soul and Thou hast filled all my being with joy.

And in this joy I have offered Thee a prayer so that it may reach up to Thee.

January 6, 1917

THOU hast filled my being with an ineffable peace and unequalled repose . . . Without any personal thought or will, I let myself be cradled passively by Thy infinity.

January 8, 1917

THOU hast made my heart and mind fall silent; but no voice has arisen from the depths of this silence. Peace alone has reigned, a sweet and beneficent guest.

January 10, 1917

DOST Thou then want to teach me that every effort that has my own being as its aim will be useless and vain? That action alone which has as its motive the radiating of Thy Grace is accomplished with ease and success. When the will acts in the external life, it is powerful and effective; when it attempts to practise going inwards, it is without force or effect. . . . So all action undertaken for personal progress becomes more and more unfruitful, and consequently rarer and rarer. On the other hand, all outer action seems to gain in effectivity what the inner has lost. Thus, O Lord, Thou takest the instrument as it is, and if it has to be refined, that will come in the course of the work.

January 14, 1917

"MAY all who are unhappy become happy, may the wicked become good, may the sick become healthy!" Thus was formulated the aspiration within me concerning the manifestation of Thy divine Love through this instrument. It was like a request, a request a child makes to its father with the certitude that it will be granted. For the certitude was in me when I asked: it seemed to me so simple and easy; I felt so clearly in myself how it was possible. To grow from joy to joy, from beauty to beauty, is this not more natural and also more fruitful than always to suffer and toil in an ignorant struggle unwillingly undergone? If Thou allowest the heart to blossom freely at the touch of Thy divine Love, this transformation is easy and comes of itself.

Wilt Thou not grant this, O Lord, as a pledge of Thy mercy?

It is with the confidence of a child that my heart implores Thee this evening.

January 19, 1917

AND the hours pass,
fading away like unlived dreams. . . .

January 23, 1917

THOU didst fill my being with so complete, so intense a love and beauty and joy that it seemed impossible to me that this would not be communicated. It was like a glowing hearth whence the breath of thought wafted far many sparks which, entering the secrecy of men's hearts, kindled other similar fires, fires of Thy divine Love, O Lord, that Love which impels and draws all human beings irresistibly to Thee. O my sweet Lord, grant that this may not be only a vision of my enrapt consciousness, but indeed a reality, effectively transforming all beings and things.

Grant that this love, this beauty and joy which flood all my being that is hardly strong enough to bear their intensity, may also flood the consciousness of all those I have seen, all those I have thought of and all those also whom I have never thought of or seen . . . Grant that all may awake to the consciousness of Thy infinite Bliss!

O my sweet Lord, fill their hearts with joy, love and beauty.

January 25, 1917

O RADIANT Love who fillest all my being and makest it festive, art Thou received, art Thou given? Nobody can say, for Thou receivest Thy own self and givest Thyself to Thyself, being sovereignly active and receptive, at once in all things, in every being.

352

January 29, 1917

IN the world of forms a violation of Beauty is as great a fault as a violation of Truth in the world of ideas. For Beauty is the worship Nature offers to the supreme Master of the universe; Beauty is the divine language in forms. And a consciousness of the Divine which is not translated externally by an understanding and expression of Beauty would be an incomplete consciousness.

But true Beauty is as difficult to discover, to understand and above all to live as any other expression of the Divine; this discovery and expression exacts as much impersonality and renunciation of egoism as that of Truth or Bliss. Pure Beauty is universal and one must be universal to see and recognise it.

O Lord of Beauty, how many faults I have committed against Thee, how many do I still commit. . . . Give me the perfect understanding of Thy Law so that I may not again fail to keep it. Love would be incomplete without Thee, Thou art one of its most perfect ornaments, Thou art one of its most harmonious smiles. At times I have misunderstood Thy role, but in the depths of my heart I have always loved Thee; and the most arbitrary and radical doctrines could not extinguish the fire of worship which, from my childhood, I had vowed to Thee.

Thou art not at all what a vain people think Thee to be, Thou art not at all attached exclusively to this or that form of life: it is possible to awaken Thee and make Thee shine in every form; but for that one must have discovered Thy secret. . . .

O Lord of Beauty, give me the perfect understanding of Thy Law, so that I may no longer fail to keep it, so that Thou mayst become in me the harmonious consummation of the Lord of Love.

March 27, 1917

(Communication in dialogue received during meditation)

"LOOK: thou seest the living form and the three inanimate images. The living one is clad in violet, the other three are made of dust, but cleansed and purified. It is in the calm of silence that the living form can, by penetrating the other three, unite them in order to transform them into a living and acting vesture."

*

O Lord, Thou knowest that I am surrendered to Thee and that my being adheres with a peaceful and deep joy to all that Thou givest it.

*

"I know thy adherence, but I would increase thy consciousness, and for that awaken what still sleeps within thee. Open thy eyes to the light, and in the limpid mirror of the mind will be reflected what thou shouldst know."

*

Lord, all is silent within my being and waits. . . .

355

"Knock at the door of consciousness and the door will be opened to thee."

*

The river runs limpid and silvery; its unbroken flow descends from the sky to the earth. But what dost Thou want to say to me that I must understand?

*

"Thy silence is not yet deep enough: something stirs within thy mind. . . .

"The fire of the soul must be seen through the veils of the manifestation; but these veils must be clear and distinct like words traced upon a luminous screen. And all this should be preserved in the purity of thy heart, as the sown meadow is shrouded and protected under the snow.

"Now that thou hast sown the seeds in the field and traced the signs on the screen, thou mayst return to thy calm silence, thou mayst go back to thy calm retreat to renew thy strength in a deeper and truer consciousness. Thou canst forget thy own person and find again the charm of the universal.

"May peace be upon thee in these hours of repose; but do not forget the reveille which will sound soon.

"Thou wilt smile yet at thy destiny which speaks to thee.

356

"Thy heart will use the returning strength.

"Thou shalt be the woodcutter who ties the bundle of firewood.

"Thou shalt be the great swan with outspread wings which purifies the sight with its pearly whiteness and warms all hearts with its white down.

"Thou wilt lead them all to their supreme destiny.

"Thou hast seen the hearth and seen the child. One attracted the other: both were happy; one because it burned, the other because it was warm.

"Thou seest it in thy heart, this triumphant hearth; thou alone canst carry it without its being destructive. If others touched it, they would be consumed. Do not let them come too near it. The child should know that it must not touch the dazzling flame which attracts it so much. From far it warms it and illumines its heart; too close, it would reduce it to ashes.

"One alone may dwell fearlessly within this heart; for he is the ray that has indeed kindled it. He is the salamander ever reborn in the fire.

"Another is above, unafraid of being burnt: it is the immaculate phoenix, the bird come from the sky who knows how to return to it.

"The first is the Power of realisation.

"The other is the Light.

"And the third the sovereign Consciousness."

*

O Lord, I listen to Thee and lie prostrate at Thy feet: Thou hast opened the door to me; Thou hast opened my eyes, and a little of the night has been illumined. . . .

358

March 30, 1917

*THERE is a sovereign royalty in taking no thought for oneself. To have needs is to assert a weakness; to claim something proves that we lack what we claim. To desire is to be impotent; it is to recognise our limitations and confess our incapacity to overcome them.

If only from the point of view of a legitimate pride, man should be noble enough to renounce desire. How humiliating to ask something for oneself from life or from the Supreme Consciousness which animates it! How humiliating for us, how ignorant an offence against Her! For all is within our reach, only the egoistic limits of our being prevent us from enjoying the whole universe as completely and concretely as we possess our own body and its immediate surroundings.*

Such too should be our attitude towards the means of action.

O Thou who dwellest in my heart and directest all by Thy supreme Will, Thou hast told me a year ago to burn all my bridges and cast myself headlong into the Unknown, as did Caesar when he crossed the Rubicon: it meant the Capitol for him or the Tarpeian Rock.

Thou didst hide then from my eyes the result of the action. Now still Thou keepest it secret; and yet Thou knowest that my equanimity remains the same before greatness as before misery.

Thou hast willed that for me the future should be uncertain and that I should go forward with confidence without even knowing where the road would lead.

Thou hast willed that I should put the care of my destiny utterly in Thy hands, and abdicate altogether all personal preoccupation.

This means undoubtedly that my road must be virgin even to my own thought.

March 31, 1917*

EACH time that a heart leaps at the touch of Thy divine breath, a little more beauty seems to be born upon the Earth, the air is embalmed with a sweet perfume, all becomes more friendly.

How great is Thy power, O Lord of all existences, that an atom of Thy joy is sufficient to efface so much darkness, so many sorrows and a single ray of Thy glory can light up thus the dullest pebble, illumine the blackest consciousness!

Thou hast heaped Thy favours upon me, Thou hast unveiled to me many secrets, Thou hast made me taste many unexpected and unhoped for joys, but no grace of Thine can be equal to this Thou grantest to me when a heart leaps at the touch of Thy divine breath.

At these blessed hours all earth sings a hymn of gladness, the grasses shudder with pleasure, the air is vibrant with light, the trees lift towards heaven their most ardent prayer, the chant of the birds becomes a canticle, the waves of the sea billow with love, the smile of children tells of the infinite and the souls of men appear in their eyes.

Tell me, wilt Thou grant me the marvellous power to give birth to this dawn in expectant hearts, to awaken the consciousness of men to Thy sublime presence, and in this bare and sorrowful world awaken a little of Thy true Paradise? What happiness, what riches, what terrestrial powers can equal this wonderful gift!

O Lord, never have I implored Thee in vain, for that which speaks to Thee is Thyself in me.

Drop by drop Thou allowest to fall in a fertilising rain the living and redeeming flame of Thy almighty love. When these drops of eternal light descend softly on our world of obscure ignorance, one would say a rain upon earth of golden stars one by one from a sombre firmament.

All kneels in mute devotion before this ever-renewed miracle.

April 1, 1917

THOU hast shown to my mute and expectant soul all the splendour of fairy landscapes: trees at festival and lonely paths that seem to scale the sky.

But of my destiny Thou didst not speak to me. Must it be so veiled from me? . . .

Once more, everywhere I see cherry trees; Thou hast put a magical power in these flowers: they seem to speak of Thy sole Presence; they bring with them the smile of the Divine.

My body is at rest and my soul blossoms in light: what kind of a charm hast Thou put into these trees in flower?

O Japan, it is thy festive adorning, expression of thy goodwill, it is thy purest offering, the pledge of thy fidelity; it is thy way of saying that thou dost mirror the sky.

And now here is a magnificent country, of high mountains all covered with pines and richly tilled valleys. And the little pink roses this Chinese brings, are they a promise of the near future?

363

April 7, 1917*

A DEEP concentration seized on me, and I perceived that I was identifying myself with a single cherry-blossom, then through it with all cherry-blossoms, and, as I descended deeper in the consciousness, following a stream of bluish force, I became suddenly the cherry- tree itself, stretching towards the sky like so many arms its innumerable branches laden with their sacrifice of flowers. Then I heard distinctly this sentence:

"Thus hast thou made thyself one with the soul of the cherry-trees and so thou canst take note that it is the Divine who makes the offering of this flower-prayer to heaven."

When I had written it, all was effaced; but now the blood of the cherry-tree flows in my veins and with it flows an incomparable peace and force. What difference is there between the human body and the body of a tree? In truth, there is none: the consciousness which animates them is identically the same.

Then the cherry-tree whispered in my ear:

"It is in the cherry-blossom that lies the remedy for the disorders of the spring."

364

April 9, 1917

ONCE the threshold of the kingdom of Thy Omniscience has been crossed, each time there is a return to the mental world, every thought one has there seems a marvellous and unfathomable problem one had never dreamed of before.

Above, no question is put; in that calm silence all is known from all eternity. Below, all is new, unknown, unexpected.

And the two meeting in one single consciousness bring a trustful wondering, source of Peace and Light and Joy.

April 10, 1917

My heart has fallen asleep down to the very depths of my being. . . .

The whole earth is in a stir and agitation of perpetual change; all life enjoys and suffers, strives, struggles, conquers, is destroyed and formed again.

My heart has fallen asleep down to the very depths of my being. . . .

In all these innumerable and manifold elements, I am the Will that moves, the Thought that acts, the Force that realises, the Matter that is put in motion.

My heart has fallen asleep down to the very depths of my being. . . .

No more personal limits, no more individual action, no longer any separative concentration creating conflict, nothing but a single and infinite Oneness.

My heart has fallen asleep down to the very depths of my being. . . .

April 28, 1917*

O MY divine Master, who hast appeared to me this night in all Thy radiant splendour, Thou canst in an instant make this being perfectly pure, luminous, translucid, conscious. Thou canst liberate it from its last dark spots, free it from its last preferences. Thou canst . . . but hast Thou not done this tonight when it was penetrated with Thy divine effluence and Thy ineffable light? It may be . . . for in me is a superhuman strength made all of calm and immensity. Grant that from this summit I may not fall; grant that peace may for ever reign as the master of my being, not only in my depths of which it has long been the sovereign but in the least of my external activities, in the smallest recesses of my heart and of my action.

I salute Thee, O Lord, deliverer of beings!

"Lo! here are flowers and benedictions! here is the smile of divine Love! It is without preferences and without repulsions. It streams out towards all in a generous flow and never takes back its marvellous gifts!"

Her arms outstretched in a gesture of ecstasy, the Eternal Mother pours upon the world the unceasing dew of Her purest love!

Akakura: July 13, 1917

ONE day I wrote:

"My heart has fallen asleep down to the very depths of my being. . . . " Merely asleep? I cannot believe it. I think it is completely hushed, perhaps for ever. From sleep one awakes, from this quietness there is no falling back. And since that day I have not observed any relapse. In place of something very intensely concentrated which for a long while was intermittently tumultuous, has come an immensity so vast and calm and untroubled, filling my being; or rather my being has melted into that; for how could that which is limitless be contained in a form?

And these great mountains with their serene contours which I see from my window, range after majestic range up to the very horizon, are in perfect harmony with the rhythm of this being, filled with an infinite peace. Lord, couldst Thou have taken possession of Thy kingdom? Or rather of this part of the kingdom, for the body is still obscure and ignorant, slow to respond, without plasticity. Will it be purified one day like the rest? And will Thy victory then be total? It matters little. This instrument is what Thou wantest it to be and its bliss is unalloyed.

Tokio: September 24, 1917*

THOU hast subjected me to a hard discipline; rung after rung, I have climbed the ladder which leads to Thee and, at the summit of the ascent, Thou hast made me taste the perfect joy of identity with Thee. Then, obedient to Thy command, rung after rung, I have descended to outer activities and external states of consciousness, re-entering into contact with these worlds that I left to discover Thee. And now that I have come back to the bottom of the ladder, all is so dull, so mediocre, so neutral, in me and around me, that I understand no more. . . .

What is it then that Thou awaitest from me, and to what use that slow long preparation, if all is to end in a result to which the majority of human beings attain without being subjected to any discipline?

How is it possible that having seen all that I have seen, experienced all that I have experienced, after I have been led up even to the most sacred sanctuary of Thy knowledge and communion with Thee, Thou hast made of me so utterly common an instrument in such ordinary circumstances? In truth, O Lord, Thy ends are unfathomable and pass my understanding. . . .

Why, when Thou hast placed in my heart the pure diamond of Thy perfect Felicity, sufferest Thou its surface to reflect the shadows which come from outside and so leave unsuspected and, it would seem, ineffective the treasure of Peace Thou hast granted me? Truly all this is a mystery and confounds my understanding.

369

Why, when Thou hast given me this great inner silence, sufferest Thou the tongue to be so active and the thought to be occupied with things so futile? Why? . . . I could go on questioning indefinitely and, to all likelihood, always in vain. . . .

I have only to bow to Thy decree and accept my condition without uttering a word.

I am now only a spectator who watches the dragon of the world unrolling its coils without end.

(A few days later)

LORD, how many times, giving way before Thy decree, I have prayed to Thee: "Spare me this calvary of earthly consciousness; let me merge in Thy supreme unity." But my prayer is faint-hearted, I know, for it remains unfruitful.

371

October 15, 1917 *

I HAVE cried to Thee in my despair, O Lord, and Thou hast answered my call.

I have no right to complain of the circumstances of my existence; are they not consonant with what I am?

Because Thou ledst me to the threshold of Thy splendour and gavest me the joy of Thy harmony, I thought I had reached the goal: but, in truth, Thou hast regarded Thy instrument in the perfect clarity of Thy light and plunged it back into the crucible of the world that it may be melted anew and purified.

In these hours of an extreme and anguished aspiration I see, I feel myself drawn by Thee with a dizzy rapidity along the road of transformation and my whole being vibrates to a conscious contact with the Infinite.

It is so that Thou givest me patience and the strength to surmount this new ordeal.

November 25, 1917*

O LORD, because in an hour of cruel distress I said in the sincerity of my faith: "Thy Will be done", Thou camest garbed in Thy raiment of glory. At Thy feet I prostrated myself, on Thy breast I found my refuge. Thou hast filled my being with Thy divine light and flooded it with Thy bliss. Thou hast reaffirmed Thy alliance and assured me of Thy constant presence. Thou art the sure friend who never fails, the Power, the Support, the Guide. Thou art the Light which scatters darkness, the Conqueror who assures the victory. Since Thou art there, all has become clear. Agni is rekindled in my fortified heart, and his splendour shines out and sets aglow the atmosphere and purifies it. . . .

My love for Thee, compressed so long, has leaped forth again, powerful, sovereign, irresistible — increased tenfold by the ordeal it has undergone. It has found strength in its seclusion, the strength to emerge to the surface of the being, impose itself as master on the entire consciousness, absorb everything in its overflowing stream. . . .

Thou hast said to me: "I have returned to leave thee no more."

And, my forehead on the soil, I have received Thy promise.

373

July 12, 1918

*SUDDENLY, before Thee, all my pride fell. I understood how futile it was in Thy Presence to wish to surmount oneself, and I wept, wept abundantly and without constraint the sweetest tears of my life. . . . *Ah yes, how refreshing, how calm and sweet were those tears I shed before Thee without shame or constraint! Was it not like a child in its father's arms? But what a Father! What sublimity, what magnificence, what immensity of comprehension! And what a power and plenitude in the response! Yes, my tears were like holy dew. Was it because it was not for my own sorrow that I wept? *Tears sweet and beneficent, tears that opened my heart without constraint before Thee and melted in one miraculous moment all the remaining obstacles that could separate me from Thee!*

Some days ago I had known it, I had heard: "If thou canst weep without restraint or disguise before Me, many things will change, a great victory will be won." And that is why when the tears rose from my heart to my eyes, I came and sat before Thee to let them flow as an offering, devotedly. And how sweet and comforting was the offering!

*And now, although I weep no longer, I feel so near, so near to Thee that my whole being quivers with joy.

Let me stammer out my homage:

I have cried too with the joy of a child, "O supreme and only Confidant, Thou who knowest beforehand all we can say to Thee because Thou art its source!

"O supreme and only Friend, Thou who acceptest,

374

Thou who lovest, Thou who understandest us just as we are, because it is Thyself who hast so made us!

"O supreme and only Guide, Thou who never gainsayest our highest will because it is Thou Thyself who willest in it!

"It would be folly to seek elsewhere than in Thee for one who will listen, understand, love and guide, since always Thou art there ready to our call and never wilt Thou fail us!

"Thou hast made me know the supreme, the sublime joy of a perfect confidence, an absolute serenity, a surrender total and without reserve or colouring, free from effort or constraint.

Joyous like a child I have smiled and wept at once before Thee, O my Well-Beloved!"*

October 10, 1918

O MY beloved Lord, how sweet it is to think that it is for Thee and Thee alone that I act! It is at Thy service that I am; it is Thou who dost decide and ordain and set in motion, guide and accomplish the action. What peace, what tranquillity, what supreme delight come with the feeling and perception of this! For it is enough to be docile, plastic, surrendered, attentive, in order to let Thee act freely; no longer then are any errors or faults, any lack or insufficiency possible, for what Thou hast willed Thou doest and Thou doest it even as Thou hast willed it. . . .

Accept the ardent flame of my gratitude and my joyous and fully confident adherence.

My father has smiled and taken me in his powerful arms. What could I fear? I have melted into Him and it is He who acts and lives in this body which He himself has formed for His manifestation.

Oiwaké: September 3, 1919*

SINCE the man refused the meal I had prepared with so much love and care, I invoked the God to take it.

My God, Thou hast accepted my invitation, Thou hast come to sit at my table, and in exchange for my poor and humble offering Thou hast granted to me the last liberation. My heart, even this morning so heavy with anguish and care, my head surcharged with responsibility, are delivered of their burden. Now are they light and joyful as my inner being has been for a long time past. My body smiles to Thee with happiness as before my soul smiled to Thee. And surely hereafter Thou wilt withdraw no more from me this joy, O my God! for this time, I think, the lesson has been sufficient, I have mounted the Calvary of successive disillusionments high enough to attain to the Resurrection. Nothing remains of the past but a potent love which gives me the pure heart of a child and the lightness and freedom of thought of a god.

(END OF THE FIRST PART)

*Pondicherry June 22, 1920**

AFTER granting me the joy which surpasses all expression, Thou hast sent me, O my beloved Lord, the struggle, the ordeal and on this too I have smiled as on one of Thy precious messengers. Before, I dreaded the conflict, for it hurt in me the love of harmony and peace. But now, O my God, I welcome it with gladness: it is one among the forms of Thy action, one of the best means for bringing back to light some elements of the work which might otherwise have been forgotten, and it carries with it a sense of amplitude, of complexity, of power. And even as I have seen Thee, resplendent, exciting the conflict, so also it is Thou whom I see unravelling the entanglement of events and jarring tendencies and winning in the end the victory over all that strives to veil Thy light and Thy power: for out of the struggle it is a more perfect realisation of Thyself that must arise.

May 6, 1927

ONE must know how to give one's life and also one's death, give one's happiness and also one's suffering, to depend for everything and in all things upon the Divine Dispenser of all our possibilities of realisation, who alone can and will decide whether we shall be happy or not, whether we shall live or not, whether we shall participate or not in the realisation.

In the integrality and absoluteness of this love, this self-giving, lies the essential condition for perfect peace, the indispensable foundation of constant beatitude.

December 28, 1928

THERE is a Power that no ruler can command; there is a Happiness that no earthly success can bring; there is a Light that no wisdom can possess; there is a Knowledge that no philosophy and no science can master; there is a Bliss of which no satisfaction of desire can give the enjoyment; there is a thirst for Love that no human relation can appease; there is a Peace that one finds nowhere, not even in death.

It is the Power, the Happiness, the Light, the Knowledge, the Bliss, the Love, the Peace that flow from the Divine Grace.

November 24, 1931*

O MY Lord, my sweet Master, for the accomplishment of Thy work I have sunk down into the unfathomable depths of Matter, I have touched with my finger the horror of the falsehood and the inconscience, I have reached the seat of oblivion and a supreme obscurity. But in my heart was the Remembrance, from my heart there leaped the call which could arrive to Thee: "Lord, Lord, everywhere Thy enemies appear triumphant; falsehood is the monarch of the world; life without Thee is a death, a perpetual hell; doubt has usurped the place of Hope and revolt has pushed out Submission; Faith is spent, Gratitude is not born; blind passions and murderous instincts and a guilty weakness have covered and stifled Thy sweet law of love. Lord, wilt Thou permit Thy enemies to prevail, falsehood and ugliness and suffering to triumph? Lord, give the command to conquer and victory will be there. I know we are unworthy, I know the world is not yet ready. But I cry to Thee with an absolute faith in Thy Grace and I know that Thy Grace will save."

Thus, my prayer rushed up towards Thee; and, from the depths of the abyss, I beheld Thee in Thy radiant splendour; Thou didst appear and Thou saidst to me: "Lose not courage, be firm, be confident, — I COME."

October 23, 1937*

(*A prayer for those who wish to serve the Divine*)

GLORY to Thee, O Lord, who triumphest over every obstacle.

Grant that nothing in us shall be an obstacle in Thy work.

Grant that nothing may retard Thy manifestation.

Grant that Thy will may be done in all things and at every moment.

We stand here before Thee that Thy will may be fulfilled in us, in every element, in every activity of our being, from our supreme heights to the smallest cells of the body.

Grant that we may be faithful to Thee utterly and for ever.

We would be completely under Thy influence to the exclusion of every other.

Grant that we may never forget to own towards Thee a deep, an intense gratitude.

Grant that we may never squander any of the marvellous things that are Thy gifts to us at every instant.

Grant that everything in us may collaborate in Thy work and all be ready for Thy realisation.

Glory to Thee, O Lord, Supreme Master of all realisation.

Give us a faith active and ardent, absolute and unshakable in Thy Victory.

Four Letters by Sri Aurobindo

I have said that the Divine does the Sadhana first for the world and then gives what is brought down to others. There can be no Sadhana without realisations and experiences. The *Prayers* are a record of Mother's experiences.

4 January 1935

*

In some of the Mother's Prayers which are addressed to "divin Maître" I find the words: "avec notre divine Mère". How can the Mother and "divin Maître" have a "divine Mère"? It is as if the Mother was not the "divine Mère" and there was some other Mother and the "divin Maître" was not the Transcendent and had also a "divine Mère"! Or is it that all these are addressed to something impersonal?

The Prayers are mostly written in an identification with the earth-consciousness. It is the Mother in the lower nature addressing the Mother in the higher nature, the Mother herself carrying on the Sadhana of the earth-consciousness for the transformation, praying to herself above from whom the forces of transformation come. This continues till the identification of the earth-consciousness and the higher consciousness is effected. The word "notre" is general, I believe, referring to all born into the earth-consciousness — it does not mean the Mother of the "Divin Maître" and myself. It is the Divine who is always referred to as Divin Maître and Seigneur. There is the Mother

383

who is carrying on the Sadhana and the Divine Mother, both being one but in different poises, and both turn to the Seigneur or Divine Master. This kind of prayer from the Divine to the Divine you will find also in the Ramayana and the Mahabharata.

21 August 1936

*

There are some Prayers of the Mother of 1914 in which she speaks of transformation and manifestation. Since at that time she was not here, does this not mean that she had these ideas long before she came here?

The Mother had been spiritually conscious from her youth, even from her childhood, upward and she had done Sadhana and had developed this knowledge very long before she came to India.

23 December 1933

*

There are many who hold the view that she was human but now embodies the Divine Mother and her "Prayers", they say, explain this view. But, to my mental conception, to my psychic being, she is the Divine Mother who has consented to put on her the cloak of obscurity and suffering and ignorance so that she can effectively lead us — human beings — to Knowledge and Bliss and Ananda and to the Supreme Lord.

The Divine puts on an appearance of humanity, assumes the outward human nature in order to tread the path and show it to human beings, but does not cease to be the Divine. It is a manifestation that takes place, a manifestation of a growing divine consciousness, not human turning into divine. The Mother was

384

inwardly above the human even in childhood, so the view held by "many" is erroneous.

> *I also conceive that the Mother's "Prayers" are meant to show us — the aspiring psychic — how to pray to the Divine.*

Yes.

17 August 1938

Note on the Text

The 313 prayers comprising this volume were selected by the Mother from her spiritual diaries. These diaries were destroyed after the selection was published. The original French text, entitled *Prières et Méditations de la Mère*, was first brought out in 1932. A second edition, which included one new prayer and an introductory note by the Mother, was issued in 1944. Subsequent editions were published in 1952, 1973, 1980 and 1990 under the shortened title *Prières et Méditations*.

An English translation of the entire text, entitled *Prayers and Meditations of the Mother*, was first published in 1948. A second edition, newly translated and with the shortened title *Prayers and Meditations*, was brought out in 1979 as Volume 1 of the Collected Works of the Mother. New impressions of that edition were issued in 1979, 1988, 1997 and 1999. The present, third edition has the same text as the second.

In 1941 English translations of sixty-one prayers (about one-fifth of the complete text) were published under the title *Prayers and Meditations of the Mother*. Six of those prayers were translated by Sri Aurobindo in their entirety, three others in part. For the rest, he revised the translations made by disciples. Further revisions were made by Sri Aurobindo when he corrected the page proofs at the time of publication. A second edition of the book, containing three more prayers added by the Mother, was issued in 1962. New editions were brought out in 1969, 1971, 1975 and 1979; the last of these editions has been reprinted several times. The sixty-four prayers in the 1962 edition were incorporated into the 1979 edition of the complete text.

For the first English edition of selected prayers, the Mother wrote an introductory note which she dated "September 1941". She recopied this note in 1948 for the first edition of the complete text in English, dating it "1941-1948"; this note is reproduced in facsimile at the beginning of this book. It is followed by an English translation of the introductory note she wrote for the 1944 (French) edition.